OLD FAMILIES

OF

STATEN ISLAND

J. J. Clute

Notice

In many older books, foxing (or discoloration) occurs and, in some instances, print lightens with wear and age. Reprinted books, such as this, often duplicate these flaws, notwithstanding efforts to reduce or eliminate them. The pages of this reprint have been digitally enhanced and, where possible, the flaws eliminated in order to provide clarity of content and a pleasant reading experience.

Originally published
New York
1877

Excerpted from:

*Annals of Staten Island, From its
Discovery to the Present Time*

Reprinted by:

Janaway Publishing, Inc.
2412 Nicklaus Dr.
Santa Maria, California 93455
(805) 925-1038
www.janawaygenealogy.com

2009

ISBN 10: 1-59641-175-9
ISBN 13: 978-1-59641-175-3

Made in the United States of America

Publisher's Preface

This book has been excerpted from *Annals of Staten Island, from its Discovery to the Present Time*, by J. J. Clute, New York, 1877, and includes pages 334 to 438 of the original volume. This work retains those original page numbers.

Janaway Publishing, Inc.

"L."

OLD FAMILIES.

THE OLD FAMILIES.

PRELIMINARY.

In preparing a history of the old families of Staten Island, it was intended at the outset to give the genealogical descents of each as full as it was possible to obtain them; we have done so, but not in the manner first proposed. Insuperable obstacles have presented themselves on every side. Two or three have declined to impart any information, probably because they knew so little of their own families, that they had none to impart, or, for some other unexplained reason. In the vast majority of instances, however, inquiries have been cheerfully answered, and every possible facility afforded, but the most of them have been unable to go further back into the past than their own grandfathers. Family bible records have afforded but little assistance, as in most cases they give only the dates of the births or deaths, or both, of individuals, without informing us what relationship they bore to other individuals mentioned in the same record, and which the families themselves are unable to trace. Other records, again, inform us that "Father A," or "Mother B," died on a certain day, without informing us whose father or mother they were, or even giving us the full name of the individual. In several instances, we have succeeded in obtaining a perfect chain of descent of some branch of a family from the original emigrant, or settlers, down to their descendants of the present day, as in the Bodine, Mersereau, Vanderbilt, Winant, and other families. Obviously, it was impossible to trace the descent of each branch of each family, for it would have been an almost interminable, and constantly accumulating labor. These, and other difficulties constantly presenting themselves, the original design was, of necessity, abandoned, and instead thereof, the reader is presented with such notices of the old members of their respective families, as we have been able to find in the records of the county, the several churches and the families themselves, leaving each to trace out his own pedigree from the materials thus furnished, if he is able. Imperfect as these notices may be, it must be gratifying to the descendants of these old families to read the names of some of their ancestors, of whom, perhaps, they never heard before.

It will be observed, that in numerous instances we give the full maiden name of the wife and mother, and the dates of the *baptisms* of the children; these are taken from the records of the Dutch church. In other instances, we give only the baptismal names of the wife and mother, and the dates of the *births* of the children; these are taken from the records of St. Andrew's Church, as are all the records of marriages.

A blank space has been left after the record of each family, for the purpose of adding, in pencil, such names as may be desired.

On Staten Island, as well as elsewhere, there are a few families whose ancestors reflect no credit on their descendants, or whose descendants reflect no credit on their ancestors; these, for obvious reasons, have been omitted.

ALSTON.

Originally this was a Scotch family; one of its most noted members was Charles Alston, a celebrated Scotch physician, and author. He died in 1760.

Joseph Alston, the son-in-law of Aaron Burr, and a former Governor of South Carolina, was also of this family.

The first of the name on Staten Island was David Alston, who came here from New Jersey, somewhere about the beginning of the Revolution. He was commissioned a Captain in the British army, his company was composed of provincial loyalists, or tories; he owned the property recently belonging to the estate of Samuel Decker, deceased, in Northfield. The large stone house in which he lived and died, was demolished a few years ago. He died between the 6th and 14th of May, 1805, for these are the dates of his will and its probate. He speaks, in that document, of his sons Warren, Japhet and David. It is said that he continued to draw his half-pay from the British Government as long as he lived.

His son Japhet, at the time of his death, which occurred July 31, 1842, at the Four Corners, Castleton, was the father of Moses Alston, Esq., late twice sheriff of the county, and of his brothers David,* Japhet, Adam,* George and William.

A copy of Captain Alston's Commission is given below, as an interesting and curious old document.

L. S. By His Excellency Sir William Howe, Knight of the most Honorable Order of the Bath, General and Commander-in-Chief of all His Majesty's Forces within the Colonies lying on the Atlantic Ocean from Nova Scotia to West Florida inclusive, &c., &c., &c.

To David Alston, Esq.:

By virtue of the Power and Authority in Me vested, I DO hereby constitute and appoint You to be a Captain of a Company in the Third Battalion of New Jersey Volunteers, Commanded by Lieut. Colonel Edward V. Dongan. You are

* Dead.

therefore to take the said Company into Your Care and
Charge, and duly to exercise the Officers as Soldiers thereof
in Arms, and to use Your best Endeavours to keep them in
good Order and Discipline from Time to Time, as you shall
receive from the General or Commander-in-Chief of His
Majesty's Forces in North America, now and for the Time
being Your Lieut.-Colonel Commandant or any other Your
Superior officer, according to the Rules and Discipline of
War in Pursuance of the Trust hereby reposed in You.

 Given under my Hand and Seal at Head Quarters in New
York, the Fifteenth day of July, One Thousand Seven Hun-
dred and Seventy-Six, in the Sixteenth Year of the Reign of
our Sovereign Lord George the Third, by the Grace of God of
Great Britain, France and Ireland king, Defender of the
Faith, and so forth.

By his Excellency's Command,   W. HOWE.
    ROBERT MACKENZIE.

ANDROVETTE.

This is one of the old families of the Island, but it was
never very prominent nor very numerous; the notices of it
therefore are few. They appear to have confined themselves
chiefly to Westfield. The name occurs nowhere in the civil
list of the county.

John is mentioned in the county records as having bought land of Tunis Egbert, Jan. 27, 1699, and as having sold land in 1705.

Peter and Rebecca Cole had the following children:

Daughter Rebecca, bap. Mar. 27, 1720.

Daughter Elizabeth, bap. Dec. 25, 1723, died in infancy.

Twins Elizabeth and Anna, bap. Jan. 1, 1726.

John and Leah Swam had son John bap. Apr. 7, 1729, and dau. Leah, bap. May 17, 1724; this John we find mentioned as collector of the West Division in 1767 and 1768. Peter and Caty his wife, had son Peter, born July 6, 1765; he made his will Dec. 21, 1792, proved Mar. 17, 1802, in which he speaks of his wife Catharine, his dau. Catharine, wife of Dow Storer; dau. Elizabeth, wife of Peter Latourette; dau. Mary, wife of Joseph Totten; sons Peter, Charles and John. These three sons were married as follows:

Peter and Elizabeth Slack, Jan. 4, 1789.

Charles and Margaret Slack, Sep. 11, 1797, and

John and Ann Cole, Aug. 21, 1802.

The family is at present represented by the three brothers, Cornelius C., John and Benjamin; their grandfather was usually known as Major John, and their father as young Major John.

BARNES.

George Barnes and Roger Barnes, brothers, came from England many years before the Revolution, but it is not certain that they came together. Roger bought land in February, 1762, in Southfield; George, about 1770, bought land in Castleton, and settled upon it. This was a large tract, lying at the southwest corner of the Turnpike and Manor Road. Constanz Brewery and the Child's Nursery occupy a part of it. Roger's wife's name was Ann, and they had a son Robert, born May, 1760, and a daughter Margaret, born April 8, 1766. George's wife's name was Dorothy, and they had the following children:

Elizabeth, born July 18, 1767.

John, born October 11, 1768.

Roger, born January 7, 1771.

They had, also, a son George.

Roger married Sally Lake, a sister of Bornt Lake, who was killed, (see Lake family,) and after the death of Roger, she married Richard Wood.

John married Margaret Perine, May 2, 1793, and they were the parents of Capt. John W. Barnes, of Port Richmond, and grandparents of Barnes Brothers, of the same place.

BEDELL.

We find this name at an early date in America, but not in connection with Staten Island. In 1673 we find Robbert Beedill, Daniel Beedel, Mathew Beedel, and John Beddell, enrolled among the inhabitants of Hempstead, Long Island. It is nearly a century after that date, that we find the name in any of the records of Richmond County. In 1768, Silas rendered a bill for "docktering," whence we infer that he was a physician. In the same year mention is made of John, who was County Treasurer when he died, in the early part of 1781. There is a Joseph also mentioned in 1770, but not the Joseph alluded to elsewhere as having been taken prisoner by the Americans when a boy ; they were father and son. The father made his will Oct. 28, 1793, proved Nov. 19, same year, in which he speaks of his sons Jesse and Joseph, and his daughters Mary, Pattie, Pegge, Catharine and Jane ; his wife's name was Catharine ; his son Joseph was born Oct. 24, 1763 ; Jesse was born 1773, and died Aug. 28, 1852.

Stephen and Catharine Latourette were mar. May, 1766, and had a son David born July 19, 1771.

Silas (the doctor) and Mary his wife, had the following children :

Phebe, born Nov. 19, 1770.

James, born Apr. 9, 1773.

John, born Mar. 28, 1775.

James married Hetty Parker Jan. 12, 1806.

There was another John, wife Catharine, who had a dau. Hillite, born Apr. 7, 1771.

Stephen and Mary Donelly were mar. Mar. 9, 1808 ; Israel died at Elizabethtown, N. J., Aug. 30, 1830 ; he was the father of the Rev. Gregory Townsend Bedell, D.D., an eminent Divine of the Episcopal Church, who was born at Fresh Kill, Oct. 28, 1793, and died Aug. 30, 1834, just four years after his father to a day. Rev. Dr. Bedell was the father of the Rev. G. Thurston Bedell ; Rev Dr. Bedell was

an only son; he was also the nephew of the late Bishop
Moore, his mother being sister of the Bishop.

BLAKE.

This family is of English origin; the date of their arrival
or settlement on the Island is not known, though it was
probably about, or just anterior to the middle of the last
century; like most of the other families of the same nation-
ality, they were decided royalists during the Revolution.
The first name of the family we find on the Records is that of
William, who married Mary Woglom, and had the following
children, viz.:

John, born Sept. 28, 1763, died Sept. 30, 1852.

William, born Apr. 21, 1766, died Jan. 16, 1852.

Edward, born ——— 1773, died Dec. 14, 1845.

John married Tabitha Merrill, and died childless.

William married Ann Corsen, and had the following children: Daniel, lately deceased, William (drowned), Richard C.
(still living in Illinois), Edward and George.

Edward was the father of Mrs. Margaret Minott, of West
New Brighton.

John, usually known as Capt. John W. Blake, owned and
occupied the now valuable property corner of Mill and Manor
roads, West New Brighton, extending westward on both sides

of Cherry Lane, and embracing the site of the Dye Works of Barrett, Nephews & Co.

William owned and occupied the property on the Little Clove road, subsequently owned by D. Porter Lord.

Daniel, son of William, recently deceased, was the father of Daniel, captain of the Police force of the county, and the present representation of the family on the Island.

BODINE.

This family is of French origin. The name is not men-. tioned by Smiles among the Huguenots. The first historical allusion to the name that we have met is, a brief biographical account of John Bodin, who was a native of Angers, studied law and lectured at Toulouse; he wrote several works, and died of the plague at Laon, in 1596. The date of the emigration of the family to this country is not known, but it must have been in the latter part of the 17th or very early in the 18th century, for we find the name of John Bodine mentioned in the county records as having purchased land in 1701, and was still living in 1744, as we find his name and that of his wife Hester mentioned as having sold land at that date. Mention is also made in records at Albany of John Bodein, in 1707. It is probable that he was an emigrant, as we find him preserving the French orthography of his name. Jean, and of his son who came with him, Francois. Jean was also a witness to a baptism in the R. D. Church, in April, 1720; he was therefore a Protestant, or Huguenot.

Francois* married Maria Dey, and they had a son named Jean, baptized in the same church Nov. 29th, 1719. Of this second Jean, or John, we find no account except that his wife's name was Dorcas, and that they had several children baptized. They were undoubtedly the parents of John Bodine, who was born in February, 1758, and of James Bodine, born in January, 1759. John died in March, 1835, nearly 82 years of age, and James in May, 1838, nearly 80 years of age. John married Catharine Britton, sister of the late Mr. Nathaniel Britton; their sons were John, usually recognized in the local history of the North Shore, as "Squire John," Jacob, (the father of W. H. J. and Edmund Bodine, constituting the present firm of Bodine Brothers, the late Capt. John, James, Jacob and Albert, and three daughters;) and Vincent, who removed from the Island. James was the father of the late Mr. Abraham Bodine, of Mariner's Harbor, and of several other sons and daughters now dead.

"Squire John" owned considerable property on the North Shore, among which was the mill, and the pond, and the land east of it, including the old Dongan Manor house, which he subsequently sold to his father, who died in that house in 1835. He also owned the property now occupied by the store of Pine, Hillyer & Co., the residence of Mr. C. M. Pine, and the dwelling west of it, in which he lived at the time of his decease.

* Vide App. N. (65.)

BOGART.

This family is of Dutch, and not of English extraction, as is generally supposed. The name was, originally, written Bogaert. The earliest mention of the name in the province occurs in an assessment roll of Breucklen (Brooklyn), dated 1678, where Theunes Gisbertse Bogaert is named, having the largest assessment on the roll. We find him again assessed in 1683. In 1715 we find the name of Simon enrolled among the militia of Kings County. Our theory is that this Simon had a brother Tunis, and that they were sons of Gysbert: for, in the assessment mentioned above, he is rated for three polls (himself and two sons); that these sons married on Long Island, the one a Ten Eyck, the other a Hageman, (for these names were common on Long, but were not found on Staten Island,) and then purchased land and removed here.

Simon Bogaert and Margarietje Ten Eyck had the following children, viz. :

A daughter Elisabet, bap. Oct. 18, 1719.

A daughter Margareta, bap. Dec. 3, 1722.

A son Simon, bap. May 19, 1726.

A son Gysbert, bap. Jan. 19, 1729.

A daughter Sarah, bap. Feb. 13, 1732, and perhaps others.

Tunis and Catharine Hegeman had the following children, viz. :

A son Isaak, bap. Nov. 2, 1718.

A son Adrian, bap. Dec. 18, 1720.

A son Abraham, bap. Apr. 21, 1723.

A daughter Maria, bap. Mar. 28, 1725.

A son Cornelius, bap. Mar. 2, 1729, and perhaps others.

Simon, (probably son of Simon,) and Martha, his wife, had the following children, viz. :

A daughter Mary, born Dec. 4, 1746.

A son Simon, born June 19, 1754.

A son Richard, born Feb. 22, 1757.

Isaac and Rachel had a son John, born Oct. 14, 1770; also

a son Simon, who was the father of the present representative
of the family on the Island, Mr. Timothy C. Bogart, near the
Four Corners.

BRAISTED.

Though this name has been identified with the county for
a century and a half, the earliest notice of it in the old
church records, is that of William and Christina Bouwman
his wife, who had a son Johannes, bap. in 1715, and a son
Andries, Aug. 18, 1719.   In the county records we meet with
him as having purchased land in 1730. Johannes, or John,
son of William, married Trintje Haughwout, and had a son
Jan, or John, bap. Aug. 18, 1741, and a son Peter, bap. Aug.
15, 1743.   We then lose trace of the family for 30 years ; then
it appears again in the name of Egbert and Rachel his wife,
who had a son Egbert, born May 6, 1773.   The next and only
remaining notice we have of the family in the last century is
the marriage of John and Nautchie (Anna) Martling,
daughter of John Martling, Feb. 14, 1790. The family is
now represented by Capt. J. Braisted, of Edgewater, and a
family or two at Watchogue, in the town of Northfield.

BRITTON.

This family is of French descent, and their name was originally written Breton, another example of the change of French names into English. The earliest mention of the name in connection with the Island, is that of Capt., sometimes called Col. Nicklos, who was born in 1679, and died Jan. 12, 1740.*

William was defendant in a suit at law Oct. 3, 1680.

Nathaniel was plaintiff in a suit in July, 1681, and again in a suit with Lewes Lakerman in the same year. These two last named were adults when "Col. Nicklos" was an infant, but the consanguinity between them cannot now be ascertained. There was another William, a son of Nicholas, probably Col. Nicklos, born Oct. 11, 1708.

There was a Joseph, perhaps a brother of William, who had a son James, bap. Apr. 23, 1707, and a daughter, in 1708.

There was also a Richard, who purchased land in 1694.

Nathaniel made his will in 1683, but he was still living in 1695; he was probably the same individual who was a party to the law-suit alluded to above.

Nathaniel and Esther Belleville had a daughter, bap. Apr. 9, 1732.

Nathaniel, and Mary his wife, had the following children :
   Joseph, born Nov. 15, 1760.
   Richard, born Mar. 22, 1766.
   William, born Sep. 19, 1768.
Samuel and Mary had the following daughters :
   Addra, born July 7, 1771.
   Mary, born July 31, 1773.
Nathaniel and Catharine had a daughter Mary, born Apr. 4, 1775; at her baptism, the father was also baptised.

Samuel and Polly Latourette, married May 24, 1797.

The present representative of one branch of the family is J. A. H. Britton, Esq., of New Dorp; his father was Nathan-

* Vide App. N. (66.)

iel, whose place of interment is marked by the marble monument at the southwest corner of the Church of the Ascension. Nathaniel was born in 1764 or '5; he was twice married; his first wife was a Van Buskirk, of Bergen, and they were the parents of Debora, wife of Joshua Mersereau, born Aug. 4, 1782, died Mar. 26, 1840; Cornelius, born July 1, 1785, died April 8, 1867; he resided at Fresh Kill for many years before his death.

Abraham, born Aug. 20, 1787, died Aug. 26, 1866; he resided on the Clove road in Castleton, and was the father of Henry and Abraham, both recently deceased, who resided on the paternal property.

Nathaniel, Jr., born in 1792, died Feb. 13, 1841; he owned and resided on the property on the east side of Broadway, West New Brighton, extending the whole length of that highway. He had also another son, John.

Nathaniel's second wife was Margaret Bedell, who was born Jan. 5, 1768, and died Sep. 21, 1849; she was the mother of J. A. H. Britton, Esq., as before mentioned.

See note, Vanderbilt family.

BURBANK.

The Burbanks are of English origin. The family tradition is that there were three brothers came to this country together, one of whom settled on Staten Island, the other two in New England, but their names and the date of their arrival has been lost. There are several branches of the family, but all are descended from the one brother, who took up his abode on the Island. John W., residing near the Four Corners, and his brother Jacob, of Tompkinsville, are the sons of Jacob, who was born April 9, 1771, and died Sept. 14, 1854. He was twice married, his first wife having been Ann Wandell, and his second Lucy Thompson, widow of —— Hennell (?) Jacob was the son of Abraham, who was born Nov. 20th, 1744, and died May 12th, 1822. Ann his wife was born June 9th, 1742, and died Nov. 24th, 1822. Their sons were Jacob, mentioned above, and Isaac, born June 17, 1787, and died Mar. 21, 1856.

The earliest mention of the name is in the baptismal record of the Ref. Dutch Church at Port Richmond, as follows: Thomas and Maritje Martling his wife had a daughter baptized April 22, 1707. Other notices of the family are found in the records of other churches and of the county.

John and Leah Haughwout his wife had a son Thomas, baptized Dec. 3, 1728, and a son John, Aug. 16, 1748.

Lucas and Martha Baile (Bailey) his wife, had children baptized between March 28, 1736, and April 13, 1742.

Peter made his will Nov. 6, 1774, which was proved Nov. 5, 1793, in which he mentions his wife Martha and his sons John, and James and his daughter Martha.

There is another Thomas mentioned in the County records 1768.

John and Elizabeth his wife had a son William, born June 3, 1786.

James and Nelly his wife had a son Abraham, born Sep. 1, 1786.

There is mention made in the County records of John, who was paid by the county for keeping his father, an invalid.

BURGHER, BURGER.

These, at the present day, are two distinct families, who write their names as above.

Johannes Burger, from Giesman, came over in the ship Stettin, Sept., 1662; but where he settled, is not known. There was an Elias Burger and Susanna Whitman, his wife, who had a son Nathan, bap. Feb. 23, 1724, and this is the first record of the name in the County.

Col. Nicholas Burgher was born Jan. 23, 1768, and died May 23, 1839; he was the father of Matthias, John, James G., David, and several other children. John was the father of Mr. David Burgher, of Edgewater, the present representative of the family spelling their name with an *h*.

The other family, who eschew the *h*, and adhere to the original orthography, are of comparatively recent connection with the Island.

David D. Burger was born in South Carolina in 1777, and settled on Staten Island in 1814, where he died in Feb., 1831. He left several sons, of whom Nicholas, of Four Corners, and Samuel, of Bull's Head, still survive.

BUSH.

This name, written *Bosch*, in the Dutch records, is found here early in the last century. The family was never very numerous nor prominent, consequently the notices of its members are very few.

Joshua, or Josiah, had a son Samuel, bap. 1706.

Nicholas and Elizabeth Drinkwater had the following children:

    Edward, bap. Nov. 24, 1728.

    Barent, bap. Sep., 1734.

    Nicholas, bap. July 13, 1740.

Garret had a daughter Mary, bap. Sep. 30, 1787, and daughter Elizabeth, bap. Aug. 30, 1789. Joseph and Mary Johnson were married Dec. 10, 1792.

Lambert and Mary Stilwell were married Jan. 27, 1795.

The family name, though not as old as some others on the Island, was in the province at an early date. Among the emigrants who came over in the ship Fox in August, 1662, we find the name of Jan Bossch from Westphalen.

There was another family of this name descended from John Bush, an Englishman, who fought at Bunker Hill on the side of the Americans, and subsequently took up his residence on Staten Island, where he married, and had at least one son, whose name was William, who was the father of the late Mr. John Bush of Watchogue, Northfield, and of Mrs. S. D. Kennison, of West New Brighton.

BUTLER.

This was another of the royalist families which were here before and during the Revolution. The earliest mention of the name in the church records is in 1732, where James and Sarah Carem had a son John, bap. Mar. 26.

In St. Andrew's records, we find the following:

Henry and Balaesha (Baletta) had a son James, born May 8, 1759; and a son Nathaniel, born Mar. 23, 1768.

Thomas and Mary had a son James, born Oct. 19, 1758, and a son Antony, born Nov. 17, 1769.

John and Rachel had a son Daniel, born Oct. 29, 1758.

John and Mary had a son Henry, bap. Mar. 11, 1776.

Thomas and Susan had a daughter Maria, bap. May 18, 1790.

Thomas and Mary Herod married Dec. 20, 1789.

Daniel and Elizabeth Pray married Dec. 29, 1807.

The family is at present in part represented by Mr. Talbot Butler, of Port Richmond, whose father was Thomas, and mother Eleanor Crocheron, daughter of Abraham; Thomas had several brothers, James, John, Elias and Henry, and they were the sons of John and —— Kingston his wife. Thomas was twice married, his second wife was a widow Blake, maiden name Wood.

William, the pioneer of Methodism on Staten Island, was born in 1769, and died 1848.

Abraham, born ——, 1751, died Feb. 19, 1798.

COLON.

James Colon, George Colon and John (elsewhere written Jonas) Colon, were naturalized May, 1770. These were probably the progenitors of the family of that name, which once were numerous, but now nearly extinct. There was also a Peter Colon in the county in 1774.

CONNER.

Richard Conner came to Staten Island from Ireland about 1760, as he purchased his landed estate at that time. He was

COLE.

We have nowhere found the slightest allusion to the origin of this family, but an individual of the same name was on the Island before the beginning of the last century; in the county records we find the name of Abraham Cole as having sold land in 1695, which, of course, he must have purchased at an earlier date. In the church records, we find no further mention of the name for more than half a century, though the name of Abraham appears to have been perpetuated.

Abraham and Hannah had a daughter Ann, born May 11, 1762.

A son Abraham, born Mar. 6, 1766, and

A son John Bedell, born July 31, 1770.

Peter and Susannah Latourette had a son Henry, born Feb. 6, 1765.

Richard lived in the county in 1766, and Cornelius in 1772.

Cornelius and Ann Dyelland were married May —— 1766.

Stephen and Ann had a daughter Ann, born July 22, 1768.

A son Stephen, born Sep. 11, 1771.

A son John, born Feb. 5, 1775, and

A daughter Margaret, who married Samuel Holmes;—see Holmes family.

Stephen, the son, married Jane Mersereau, Oct. 16, 1796, and John, the son, married Mary Winant, Apr. 1, 1797.

Isaac and Esther his wife, had a son Edward, born Apr. 8, 1770.

Richard and Mary Spragg were married Oct., 1774.

Richard and Mary his wife, had a son Abraham, born Mar. 6, 1775.

John and Catharine his wife, had a son Abraham, born Apr. 6, 1775.

Cornelius and Frances Cole were married Nov. 11, 1797.

John and Eliza Drake were married Dec. 24, 1801.

only shreds of its history, none of those now bearing the name being in possession of a genealogical descent. From 1650 to 1690, we find the names of Hendrick, Peter, Jan, Philip, &c., as residents of New York, or some parts of Long Island. The first mention of the name in connection with Staten Island occurs Dec. 30, 1680, in a patent bearing that date, conveying to Cornelius Corsen, Andries Juriansen, Derrick Cornelison and John Peterson, 180 acres of land, 60 acres of which belonged to Corsen, and 40 acres to each of the others. This land is referred to in the patent of Gov. Dongan to Palmer, and mentioned as the land belonging to Cornelius Corsen and company. Another patent to the same parties, of the same date, conveyed 320 acres of land lying westward of, and bounded by the Mill Creek, beside 32 acres of salt meadow " where most convenient." This Cornelius is designated as Captain in a record in Albany, dated Dec. 21, 1680. We find him mentioned again in the county records as being plaintiff in a suit in January, 1681. He died before Dec. 7, 1693, as his will was proved on that day, before "Benjamin Fletcher, Captain-General and Governor-in-chief of the province of New York, province of Pennsylvania, county of Newcastle, and the territories and tracts depending thereon in America." By this will he devises his property to his wife Maritje for her life, and then to be equally divided among his children. He had at least three sons; Christian, 2d Judge and Lt. Col. in 1738, Cornelius, a justice, and Jacob, who made his will Oct. 8, 1742, by which he makes the following bequests: his homestead to his son Jacob, £70 ($175) to his daughter Suster, wife of Johannes Simonson; £70 to his daughter Mary, wife of Joshua Mersereau; £70 to his son Douwe; £70 to his son Benjamin; £70 to his daughter Rebecca, wife of John Blom; to his sons Douwe and Benjamin all his lands in Hunterdon county, N. J.; to his daughter Suster all his lands on the west side of Staten Island, meaning the land mentioned in his father's patent as lying west of the Mill Creek, on which some of the Simonson family, her descendants, still reside; to his son Jacob his silver-hilted

sword and silk sash,* and all his other goods to his children
equally.

Daniel Corsen, who was County Clerk in 1739, was probably
another son of Capt. Conelius.

In the church-yard of the Reformed Church at Port Richmond, there are still to be seen two head-stones, with the
following inscriptions in the Dutch (Holland) language:

Hier onder rust het lyk. van
CORNELIUS CORSEN, Esq.,
overleden den 26 Maart—
A. D. MDCCLV on—
—ynde LIII.

Here under rests the body of
CORNELIUS CORSEN, Esq.,
who died the 26 March, 1755,
in his 53d——

———

Hier legt het Lighaam van
JANNETIA VAN BOSKERK,
Huys vrouw van Cornelius
Corsen——
Overleeden den——
MDCCXLIX——
Zyude L Jaar——

Here lies the body of
JANE VAN BUSKIRK,
wife of Cornelius Corsen——
died the ——, 1749, in her 50th year.

This good old lady was probably a native of Bergen, N. J.,
where there were several families of the Van Buskirks,
there being none of that name on the Island at that date.
She was born in 1699, three years before her husband, a sub-
ject of William and Mary; she was three years old when
Queen Anne began to reign; she was fifteen years old when
George I. was crowned, and twenty-eight when George II.

* Vide App N. (67.)

ascended the throne, and had been dead eleven years when George III. succeeded to the crown; she had children older than George Washington, who was seventeen when she died; she had been dead twenty-seven years when the United States were declared independent. She has slumbered in her tomb a hundred and twenty-seven years, all unconscious of the mighty events which have transpired during that period; strangers have trodden in her paths for more than a century and a quarter; her country's foemen, with ruthless foot, have desecrated her tomb, but she heeded nothing, and slept on as unconcerned as if all had been as peaceful and quiet as her own slumbers.

Cornelius and Jannetje Van Buskirk had the following children:

A daughter, bap. Nov. 24, 1723.

A son Peter, bap. Aug. 18, 1725.

A son Christian, bap. Feb. 26, 1727.

A son Cornelis, bap. Feb. 23, 1729, died an infant.

A son Cornelis, bap. Feb. 21, 1731.

A son Jacobus (Jacob), bap. Oct. 22, 1732.

A son Daniel, bap. Mar. 9, 1735, died May 22, 1801.

A daughter, bap. Sep. 19, 1736.

A daughter, bap. Sep. 23, 1738.

We append the following, collected chiefly from church records:

Cornelius, son of Benjamin, bap. May 4, 1714.

Daniel, born 1714, died Jan. 26, 1761.

Capt. Jacob, born 1707, died 1772.

Benjamin and Blandina Vile (Viele) had a son Benjamin, bap. Aug. 8, 1718.

Jacob and Cornelia Cruser had the following children:

Jacob (see note) bap. Oct. 13, 1747, and three daughters, between 1739 and 1754.

Douwe (son of Jacob) and Jannetje Cosin, had a child bap. Oct. 5, 1755.

Daniel and Maria Stilwell had sons Richard and Daniel, both bap. Nov. 7, 1753.

Cornelius, Jr., had son Cornelius, bap. Sep. 2, 1787, and a daughter Jannetje (Jane), bap. Oct. 17, 1790.

Richard had a daughter Catharine, bap. Aug. 30, 1789.

Daniel and Elizabeth Bogart, had son Cornelius, bap. Sep. 17, 1758, and son William Howe, born Nov. 24, 1776.*

Jacob had a daughter, bap. Mar. 25, 1701, a son Jacob, bap. Oct. 21, 1707, (see Capt. Jacob, above) and a son Benjamin, bap. Apr. 1, 1710.

—————— Corsen and Elsey Ayro mar. Nov., 1801.

Hiram J., of New Springville, is the son of Cornelius V. B.; he was the son of Richard; and he was the son of Cornelius.

Note.—We copy, as a curiosity, an inscription on a gravestone in the Port Richmond Ref. Church grave-yard, as follows:

"Her legt het lighaam van Jacob Corsen, Zoon Van Jacob A. Corsen, Jun', Deezer Werreld overleeden den 6: 9 ber: 1748 oud zynde 15 Manden en 14 Dagen."

Here lies the body of Jacob Corsen, son of Jacob A. Corsen, Jun., who departed this world November 6, 1748, 15 months and 14 days old.

This was undoubtedly the infant son of Jacob and Cornelia, whose baptism is noticed in the text.

---

* Daniel and Elizabeth Bogart his wife, had also three other sons, John, Daniel and Richard; Richard married Elizabeth Egbert, and they were the parents of Mr. Abraham E. Corsen, of Mariner's Harbor. Daniel built the stone-house still standing near the Richmond Turnpike, and now the property of A. C. Bradley, Esq.; subsequently he owned a farm on the Clove road, now or recently the property of Haynes Lord, Esq., where he died, and the place came into the possession of his son Richard. William Howe Corsen lived to have a family of his own; a short time previous to the war of 1812, he was murdered, and his body concealed under a bridge on the public road. Evidently he had been robbed. The perpetrators of the crime were never detected.

CORTELYOU.

This name, in some of the old records, is written Corteleau ; it is of French origin, but changed through a long residence in Holland, previous to emigration to America. The family was in this country at an early date ; Jacques Cortelliau (so written by himself,) was the surveyor, who, in 1657, laid out the town of New Utrecht, on Long Island, into 20 lots, of 50 acres each, one of which was assigned to him for his residence. He came to America in 1652, for in 1687, when the inhabitants of Kings County took the oath of allegiance to James II, the name of Jaques Corteljou is found among them, with a note attached, that he had then been in the country 35 years. He had four sons, all of whom had been born on Long Island ; their names were Jacques, Jr., Cornelis, Pieter, Willem ; still, in the assessment roll of New Utrecht, for the year 1676, neither of their names appear. The family on Staten Island is undoubtedly descended from that of Long Island, though when the removal took place, is uncertain ; a part of them remained on Long Island, as in 1738 we find the names of "pijeter kartelijou," and "ailte kartelijou," still at New Utrecht. The first mention of the name in the church records on Staten Island, is that of Jaques, and his wife Jacomyntie (Jemima) Van Pelt, who had a daughter Debora, bap. Dec. 26, 1720. Aaron, who was born 1726, and died Aug. 22, 1789, was undoubtedly the son of Jacques and Jacomyntie, as they appear to have been the only family of the name on Staten Island. Aaron had a son Peter, born Dec. 27, 1768, and died Feb. 3, 1857, and he was the father of the present representative of the family, Judge Lawrence H., of Fresh Kill. Aaron was one of the original members of the Moravian Church. There was a Jacob, probably a brother of Peter, born Aug. 26, 1760, and died Feb. 7, 1817. There is a record of a Peter, who married Sarah Van Pelt, Dec. 31, 1801.

CRIPS.

This family can scarcely be numbered among the old families of the county, though at one time they were tolerably numerous ; they are now almost extinct. The earliest notice we have found in the marriage of John Crips and Margaret Bety (Beatty) Jan. 5, 1761, they had a son William, born Apr. 28, 1764.

William and Sarah had daughter Elizabeth, bap. June 23, 1771.

Thomas and Mary Perine were married Nov. —, 1791.

James and Elizabeth Blake were married Oct. 1, 1801.

There was a Richard, mentioned in the county records in 1766.

CROCHERON.

One branch of this family, which once was numerous, but is now disappearing, is represented by Mr. Daniel G. Crocheron, of Graniteville; Mr. Abraham Crocheron, of New Springville, represents another branch, both having descended from the same original progenitor. Joseph, Daniel G., Abraham, Stephen, David and George, were the sons of Daniel Crocheron and Eliza Wood his wife, who were married August

3, 1791. Daniel was the son of Abraham and Margaret his wife, and was born Jan. 15, 1770. Abraham was the son of Daniel and Maria Dupuy his wife, and was baptised March 30, 1740, and died June 28, 1806. Mr. Abraham Crocheron, of New Springville, is the son of Abraham, who was born Jan. 6, 1790, and he was the son of Abraham and Jane his wife.

The first mention of the family in the county records is of John, in 1698; subsequently, but in the same year, mention is made of Nicholas, so that there were two individuals of the name of Crocheron in the county at that early date, but we have no means of knowing in what degree of relationship they stood to each other, if any. Henry Crocheron and Nannie his wife had the following sons: John, born April 13, 1770; Henry, born Dec. 26, 1772; Jacob, born August 28, 1774, (he married Mary Oakley, Feb. 22, 1797; he was Sheriff of the County, etc.,) and Reuben, baptized September 24, 1789. Abraham Crocheron and Elizabeth his wife had a son Nicholas, born August 9, 1761, and died December 30, 1817, (he was familiarly known as "Squire Nick,") Henry, born March 22, 1766.

There was another Abraham, and Margaret his wife, who had a son Daniel, born January 15, 1770.

Daniel and Sarah his wife had a daughter Mary, born April 8, 1775.

John Crocheron and Jenny his wife, had a daughter Mary, born March 4, 1773.

Abraham and Mary Prall his wife had a son Abraham, born Sept. 4, 1787, and a son Benjamin, baptized June 28, 1789. (Benjamin died a few years ago on the Old Place Road; his wife was Susannah Prall, his cousin. Abraham, the father, formerly owned the farm now a part of New Brighton).

Another Daniel had a son Daniel born June 9, 1788.

John and Hannah Housman were married February 10, 1792.

Daniel and Jane Jones were married November 29, 1798.

Nicholas and ——— Winant were married May 28, 1801.

The Crocheron family have been prominent in the county; Henry was Member of Congress 1815—'17. Jacob was Mem.

ber of Congress 1829—'31 ; Presidential elector in 1836 ;
Sheriff 1802, 1811 and 1821.

Nicholas was Member of Assembly, 1854.

Richard was County Treasurer, and Surrogate, 1836, and
for several years thereafter.

The family is of French descent.

CRUSER.

CRUISE, CROES, KROESEN, &c. The family is of Dutch
descent.

It is impossible now to ascertain when Garret, who is probably the first of the name in America, emigrated. In 1676,
we find him rated in Breucklyn, but after that date his name
does not appear among the freeholders of that place. It is
probable that he removed to Staten Island the following year,
for then Sir Edmond Andross granted him a patent for 160
acres of land on Staten Island. On Long Island he had but
28 acres. He had, probably, the following sons, Hendrick,
Cornelius, Dirk or Derick, Garret and Jan. Hendrick, who
was perhaps the eldest, had several children baptized on
Staten Island between 1698 and 1716. Cornelius married
Helena Van Tuyl, probably a daughter of Otto Van Tuyl,
and had the following children baptized here :

Hendrick, Oct. 10, 1731.

Abraham, July 29, 1733, died March 11, 1770.

Cornelius, Aug. 8, 1736.

Derick had the following children baptized here:

Nicklas, May 6, 1696.

Derick, Oct. 22, 1701.

Hendrick, July 8, 1707.

Garret had the following children baptized here:

Cornelius, Oct. 28, 1711.

Derick, Oct. 18, 1713.

Garret, April 1, 1717.

Jan had a daughter Elizabeth, baptized July 14, 1713.

Cornelius, son of Cornelius and grandson of Garret, married Beeltje de Groot, and had a son Cornelius, baptized Aug. 26, 1759.

Abraham, son of Cornelius, and grandson of Garret, married Antye Simonson, and had a son Johannes, or John, baptized June 4, 1760.

(This John had a daughter Elizabeth, baptized May 10, 1789.)

Garret, son of Garret and grandson of the original Garret, married Claartje (Clara, Clare, Clarissa) Blencroft, and had a daughter Cornelia, baptized Aug. 27, 1740; a daughter Clarissa, baptized Oct. 11, 1748, and a son Hendrick June 24, 1752, and others.

Garret, son of Hendrick and grandson of the original Garret, married Gertrude Van Tuyl, and had the following children:

Hendrick, baptized Dec. 8, 1723.

Femitje (Euphemia ?) Sept. 13, 1728.

Abraham, Aug. 6, 1732.

The late Morris H. Cruser and brothers are the direct descendants of John, mentioned above.

The family were once numerous and prominent, but like many other of the old families, is disappearing.

CUBBERLY.

This family is of English descent, but came to Staten Island from New Jersey. The name originally was written Coverle, but by some unaccountable metamorphosis, has become so changed that the owners of the original name, were they living, would not recognize their own legitimate descendants.

The first of the name on Staten Island was Isaac, who resided here in 1769. Probably he came here a young man, for he married here, in the Journeay family. His sons were Stephen, Joseph, James, Thomas and Isaac. Isaac married an English woman named Broughton, and had two sons— William, now living in New Jersey, and James, once clerk of the county ; Mrs. Charles E. Racy, of West New Brighton, is also his daughter. Isaac resided at the noted locality known as "The Elm Tree," where, though a large part of his property is now submerged by the waters of the ocean, his dwelling house still stands.

There is another branch of the family which we are unable to trace, viz. : Joseph and Auder (*sic*) his wife had a son James, born Oct. 18, 1776 ; this James married Eleanor Ralph, January 20, 1799. The late William Cubberly, of Port Richmond, is descended from this branch.

DECKER.

This family is by far the most numerous, as well as one of the oldest, on the Island. Its progenitor was Johannes De Decker, who arrived here in April, 1655. He was a prominent man in the colony, filling various offices of responsibility, and after a public service of many years, finally settled down for the remainder of his life on his farm of 120 acres, on Staten Island. His numerous descendants have so frequently intermarried, that at this day it is worse than useless to attempt to trace their genealogy. Some of the elder members retained the prefix De, but it has long ago fallen into disuse. Mattheus De Decker, probably a son of Johannes, had

A son John, bap. Sep. 7, 169—.

A son Abraham, Oct. 21, 1707.

A daughter Elizabeth, Apr. 17, 1711, and

A son Mattheus, ——, 1715 ; to this baptism Pieter De Decker was sponsor, who was also probably a son of Johannes.

This Pieter and Susanna Hetfeel (Hatfield,) his wife, had the following children baptized :

A daughter Maria, Sep. 21, 1718.

A son Johannes, July 24, 1720.

A daughter Susanna, May 24, 1724.

A daughter Sara, Oct. 23, 1726.

A son Mattheus, June 10, 1728.

A daughter Eva, Mar. 26, 1732, and

A son Abraham, Apr. 7, 1735.

John—probably a son of Mattheus—and Maria Swaim, had a daughter bap. July 3, 1726, Charles Decker, sponsor, who was probably another son of Johannes.

John (son of Pieter) and Nancy, or Anna Merrell, had

A son Johannes, bap. Apr. 19, 1743, and

A son Richard, Apr. 26, 1748.

Charles, (above mentioned,) and Lena Swaim, had

A son Matthys, bap. Apr. 5, 1730, died in infancy.

A son Mattheus, bap. Mar. 16, 1733, and

A daughter, Jan. 8, 1738.

Richard, known as Col., born May 15, 1747, died May 26, 1817; his mother was a Merrill (see above), and his wife was Wyncha Merrill. They had a son Richard, bap. Oct. 26, 1788.

Matthew, (son of Charles) and Merrian, his wife, had

A son Israel, bap. Aug. 28, 1763, and Israel had a daughter bap. Feb. —, 1788.

John (son of John, above) and Elizabeth, his wife, had

A son Reuben, born Aug. 6, 1766, and

Reuben and Mary Swaim were married July 25, 1790.

Abraham and Phebe his wife had

A son Noah, born Mar. 26, 1773, and

A son Charles, born Apr. 10, 1775.

Moses and Elizabeth Wood were married April, ——, 1769.

Matthias and Lidde (Lydia) Milburn were married Nov. ——, 1775.

Isaac and Margaret Jones were married Aug. 7, 1791.

Jacob and Leah Depue were married June 5, 1796.

Sylvanus and Sarah Parker were married Oct. 24, 1800.

Isaac and Elizabeth Christopher were married Oct. 13, 1804.

Matthew made his will Apr. 26, 1787, proved Sep. 15, 1787, in which he mentions his wife Catharine, son of Matthew, a minor, and daughters Margaret, Elsie, Elizabeth, Ann and Catharine, who was lame.

Hon. John Decker, of Port Richmond, represents one branch of this family; his brothers were Matthias, Benjamin and David, the two first deceased. Their father was David, and their mother Catharine Decker; David's brothers were John, Benjamin and Abraham; they were the sons of Benjamin and Mary Egbert, and Benjamin was the son either of Matheus, son of Charles, or Mattheus son of Pieter, probably the latter.

DE GROOT.

This family, though originally French, and known as Le Grand, for centuries past has been regarded as Dutch, the name by which it is now known being simply a translation of the French name. The eminent scholar and advocate, Hugo de Groot, otherwise known as Grotius, was a member of this family. Motley, in his life of John of Barneveld, says of him: "He was then (June 5th, 1619) just 36 years old. Although comparatively so young, he had been long regarded as one of the great luminaries of Europe for learning and genius. Of an ancient and knightly race, his immediate ancestors had been as famous for literature, science and municipal abilities, as their more distant progenitors for deeds of arms in the feudal struggles of Holland in the middle ages. His father and grandfather had alike been eminent for Hebrew, Greek and Latin scholarship, and both had occupied high positions in the University of Leyden from the beginning. Hugo, born and nurtured under such quickening influences, had been a scholar and poet almost from his cradle. He wrote respectable Latin verses at the age of seven; he was matriculated at Leyden at the age of eleven. When fourteen, he took his bachelor's degree. On leaving the University, he was attached to the embassy of Barneveld, and Justinus van Nassau to the Court of Henry IV. In France, before he was fifteen, he received from the University of Orleans the degree of Doctor of Laws. At seventeen he was an Advocate in full practice before the Supreme tribunals of the Hague, and when twenty-three years old he was selected by Prince Maurice from a list of three candidates for the important post of Fiscal or Attorney-General of Holland. At twenty-six he published Mare Liberum—a little later, his work on the Antiquity of the Batavian Republic. At twenty-nine he had completed his Latin History of the Netherlands. His great work on the Rights of War and Peace was afterwards written." * * *

There were two emigrants of this name to America, viz.,

Willem Pietersen de Groot, wife and five children, came over in April, 1662, in the ship called the "Hope;" and Staes de Groot, who came over in the "Spotted Cow," the succeeding April.

The name is not found in any of the old State documents, except upon Staten Island and in Albany county. The emigrants settled in these places, the latter on Staten Island. The earliest notice in our local records is as follows :

Johannes (a son of Staes) and Elizabeth Seckkels his wife had the following children:

Peter, bap. April 2d, 1729.

Robert, bap. Oct. 10th, 1731.

Johannes, bap. Feb. 1st, 1735.

Peter married Claartje (Clare) Post, and had the following children:

Garret, bap. Aug. 25th, 1751.

John, bap. May 2d, 1753.

Katrina, bap. July 27th, 1755.

Gertrude, bap. July 17th, 1758.

John, son of Peter, married Mary Wood, and they were the parents of Jacob de Groot, who died March 11th, 1875, aged 86 years, and grand-parents of Alfred de Groot, the present representative of the family in this county.

DE HART.

Of the ancestors of this family on the Island, there is but little to be learned from the local records; what we have been able to glean is as follows:

Daniel had a son Daniel, bap. Oct. 22, 1707.

A daughter ——, April 17, 1711.

A son Matthias, bap. ——, 1815.

A son Samuel, bap. 1717, died May 17, 1798.

Baltus and Mary Phillipse, had daughter Catalyn, bap. 1746 or –'7.

Matthias, born Aug. 21, 1749; died Oct. 20, 1840.

Edward had a son Jacob, bap. Oct. 24, 1790.

———

DEPUY.

DEPUY, PEW, DUPUE, DEPEUE, DEPEW, &c.

At the Revocation of the Edict of Nantes, there was a Protestant family of this name in Languedoc. Two brothers of this family, Philip and David, then fled to Holland, and became officers in the army of William of Orange; they accompanied him to England, and were both killed at the battle of the Boyne. Another brother, Samuel, was an officer in the British army, and served in the Low Countries. But some of the name were in America before the Revocation. In 1662, Nicolas du Pui, with his wife and three children, came to this country in the ship called the "Purmerland Church;" he probably settled on Staten Island, and was the

progenitor of the family here, as we find his baptismal name
perpetuated among them. If this assumption is correct, then
the names of two of the three children were John and Francis,
for we find them mentioned in the public records as early as
1680; John as defendant in a suit in March of that year, and
Francis as owning a tract of woodland near Fresh Kill, in
December of that year.   We do not meet with the name of
Francis after that date, but find the name of John again, in
the church record, as having a daughter Elizabeth baptized
Oct. 22, 1707, and a son Moses, July 22, 1714.

Nicolas, perhaps a grandson of the original, and Neeltje
(Cornelia) Dekker had the following children :

A daughter, bap. Apr. 6, 1724.

A son, John, bap. June 27, 1725.

A son, Matthew, bap. Oct 8, 1726.

A son, Nicolas, bap. June 4, 1730.

A son, Moses, bap. Oct. 27, 1732.

A son, Aaron, bap. Aug. 26, 1739.

Nicholas, last mentioned, was supervisor of Westfield,
1766, &c.

John, last mentioned, and his wife Sarah, had a son Nicholas, bap. ——, 1757.

Moses, last mentioned, and his wife Leah, had the following children :

John, born Jan. 10, 1759.

Nicholas, born June 8, 1766.

Moses, born Jan. 17, 1769.

Barent, who probably was another son of Nicolas, and
Neltje, and his wife Elsie Poillon, had the following children :

Martha, bap. May 20, 1750.

Elsie, bap. Dec. 9, 1739.

There was a Barent, who made his will June 4, 1792, which
was probated Aug. 17, 1792, in which he speaks of his wife
Mary, and the following children : Nicholas, Barent, Daniel,
Abraham, Mary, Elsie, Sally and Elizabeth.   These two
named Barents may be identical, but if so, he was twice married, and his daughter Martha was dead when he made his
will.

DISOSWAY.

The name of Du Secoy is found among the Huguenot families who left France before the Revocation of the Edict of Nantes. It has been ascertained, from the State records, that Marcus, Job, Peter, Israel, and Susanne, settled on Staten Island, opposite Perth Amboy, more than two centuries ago. The name of Marcus is mentioned in the colonial history in 1678, petitioning for men to be sent to Court at Fort William Henry. A portion of the land originally purchased by this family (500 acres), and the stone house erected upon it, is still owned and occupied by some of the descendants. Like many other French names, unpronounceable to English and Dutch tongues, this has undergone various changes in the course of two hundred years. In the Dutch Church baptismal records, the oldest and most reliable authority, it is always written Du Secoy and Du Secay. In the County records, often copied by careless or illiterate clerks, the name is spelled Dus Souchoy, Dusway, Dusuchoy, Dussoway, Dessoway, Dusosway, Disosway. The fact that the original emigrants were Huguenots, is evidence of their individual piety, and it is said that, during the war of the Revolution, though surrounded by enemies, they were firm in their adherence to the cause of their country.

There are several of the name mentioned in the County records as having purchased land as early as 1687. The following are taken from old church records:

Marcus Du Secoy had a son Gabriel, bap. Apr. 20, 1708, at which Susanna Du Secoy was sponsor; these were, probably, two of the original emigrants. As there was no Gabriel among them, it was the Gabriel whose baptism we have just noticed, who was sponsor at the baptism of his relative's (probably sister's) child, in Jan., 1725, when Dina Du Secoy, wife of Henrick Bries, had a daughter baptized; she had had a son Henrick baptized three years previous.

Israel, and Gertrude Van Deventer, his wife, had a daughter baptized June 3, 1722.

Job, and Sara Deny, his wife, had a son Johannes baptized September 22, 1723.

Cornelius, and Catharine, his wife, had a daughter Ann, baptized December 9, 1757.

Mark and Eliza Cortelyou married November 2, 1790.

DUBOIS.

Sometimes written DUBOYS, DEBAA, &c.

This was a large family, some of them residing in Brittany, and some in French Flanders.   Antoine Dubois, and some of his relatives, fled to England as early as 1583, to escape persecution for their religious opinions.   It is not known when the family first came on the Island, nor who was the first of the name; the earliest name mentioned in the church record is that of Louis du Bois, Jun., whose wife's name was Catharine Van Brunt; they had a son Samuel who was baptised Dec. 11, 1737.   They had also a son Benjamin, and a son John.   Benjamin became a minister of the Reformed Dutch Church in 1764, and was immediately settled over the churches of Freehold and Middletown, N. J., where he remained sixty-three years.

John and Hester his wife had a daughter Mary, born June 27, 1766; he made his will Jan. 17, 1793, which was proved Feb. 1, 1794, in which he speaks of his wife Hester; his daughters, Hester, wife of Lewis Prall; Martha, wife of Daniel Winants; Elizabeth, wife of Charles Laforge; and Mary, wife of James Laforge, and his son Richard.

There was another John who had a son, Nathaniel R., and died at the age of 87 ; his son, Nathaniel, died in May, 1874, age 85 years ; his wife was Frances Butler.

Lewis and Jane Mersereau married Jan. 12, 1804.

The family, once tolerably numerous and highly respectable, are almost extinct in the county.

———

DUSTAN.

This family has for many years been identified with the Island. William and Peter were natives of Scotland, and emigrated to America at an early age. The former, locally known as Major Dustan, was born September 11th, 1759, and died on Staten Island, May 23d, 1841, nearly 82 years of age. He left one son, Isaac Kip, whose melancholy death is recorded on his monument in the Moravian Cemetery, as follows:

"This monument is erected a tribute of esteem to the memory of Isaac Kip Dustan, aged 38 years and 7 months, who lost his life while in the discharge of his duties as Captain of the ill-fated Steamer Atlantic, off Fisher's Island, during the memorable gale of the 28th of November, 1846."

The monument is surmounted by a marble bell, on which is the following epitaph.

"Far, far o'er the waves, like a funeral knell,
Mournfully sounds the Atlantic's bell.
Tis the knell of the dead, but the living may hear :
Tis a warning to all, mid the opening year.
In the midst of our life, as we draw out each breath,
How swiftly we haste to the caverns of death ;
May the fate of the lost one our own warning be
Like a death-knell rung out o'er life's treacherous sea."

Capt. Dustan was a man of powerful frame, with a commanding presence, and a universal favorite. He married a daughter of the late Charles M. Simonson, and left one son, Charles, who, during the late rebellion, entered the Union army as a private, and gradually rose to the rank of Brigadier-General. He is now a resident of the State of Alabama, and a member of its Legislature. The wife of Geo. J. Greenfield, Esq., of Edgewater, is also his daughter.

EDDY.

The present representatives of this family are Cornelius C., of Stapleton, and his cousin James, of Huguenot, in Westfield. The former is the son of William, who was killed by his horse running away, in January, 1828; the latter is the son of John, also deceased. William, John and Andrew, who is still living near Wood-row church, Westfield, were brothers and sons of William, the first of the name, who came here from New Jersey, during the war of the Revolution, with the intention of remaining but a short time; but either the refusal of a pass, or protracted delay in furnishing it, detained him on the Island, until finally, having probably formed some attachment, he relinquished the idea of returning, and settled permanently.

EGBERT.

The first emigrant of this name was probably Govert Egbert, who came to America in the ship called the "Spotted Cow," in 1660, but it is not certain that he ever lived on Staten Island.

The first mention of the name in connection with the Island, is that of Tunis, who bought land in 1698, and sold land to John Androvat in January, 1699. The tradition, in one branch of the family, is that some of the grandsons of this Tunis are still living, which is improbable, unless we accord to him an extraordinary length of life, as well as to his son Johannes or John. If this Tunis married Petronella Dupuy, then his son John was bap. Dec. 1745, and his sons, in the order of their birth, were Joseph, John, Tunis, Samuel, Edward, Thomas, Holmes, Cornelius, Henry, and William. Of these are still living (1876) Edward, on the Manor road, Castleton ; Cornelius,* on the Amboy road, Southfield, and William at Graniteville. If the above is reliable, then probably the same Tunis had another son named Abraham, (born Sep. 21, 1747, died Oct. 2, 1816), who was father of the following sons, viz.: Abraham, Joseph, Tunis, Cornelius, John, Stephen, James and Edward ; two sons and seventeen grandsons, besides grand-daughters and daughters, whose names are not given. We subjoin the following, indiscriminately, as we have collected them from several records.

James is mentioned in the county records in 1724, and again in 1766.

Peter is also mentioned in 1767.

Tunis, probably a son of the original Tunis, born 1720, and died May 19, 1805.

Tunis born Jan. 11, 1759, died Nov. 5, 1825.

Moses and his wife Caty had a son Abraham, born Nov. 8, 1768, "about 3 o'clock."

* Vide App. N. (68.)

Moses, the above, was born Oct. 21, 1742, and died Nov. 13, 1831.

Jacus (James?) and Trientje Backer (Baker?) had a daughter bap. Oct. 11, 1743.

Abraham and Elizabeth Gerresen had a daughter bap. Apr. 17, 1744, and a son Benjamin, born Aug. 25, 1768.

Abraham and Francyntje Parain (Francina Perine) had a son Abraham, born May 22, 1715; a son John, bap. Apr. 10, 1720; a daughter Elizabeth, bap. June 17, 1722.

Jacobus (James) and Catharine Deny had a son Johannes, bap. July 14, 1723; a son Laurens, bap. Mar. 24, 1724.

Jaques and Catharine Bakker (Baker?) had a daughter Susannah, bap. Nov. 4, 1733, identical with the above Jacus.

Anthony and his wife Mary had a son Reuben, born Sep. 13, 1770, "on Thursday, about 10 of the clock in y° Morning."

A daughter Martha, "born April 25 about 10 of y° clock in y° morning, 1772, on Saterday."

A daughter Eleanor, "born Aug. 7 about one of y° clock in y° morning 1774."

John and Catharine his wife had twins, Tunis and Eleanor, born Nov. 11, 1771."

Barney and Ann Taylor married Oct. 4, 1801.

ENYARD.

In the County records is found the name of Jollis Inyard, who purchased land on the Island as early as 1687, and sold land in 1692. In 1708 the same individual, under the name of Yellis Ingart, sold land. The names Jollis, Yellis, and Gillis are the same, being Dutch corruptions of Giles. He had a son Matthys, (Matthias) whose wife was Elizabeth Gerritson, and they had the following children:

Matthys,* bap. Jan. 7, 1730.

Gillis, bap. Dec. 17, 1732.

Susanna, bap. May 4, 1735.

Catharine, bap. Apr. 23, 1739.

Elisabet, bap. Apr. 18, 1743.

Nicklaes, bap. Apr. 22, 1746.

Nicholas married Jemima Wood, July ——, 1768. They had a son Elias, who was the father of Mr. John Enyard, of Port Richmond, and grand-father of Rev. William T. Enyard, pastor of the Ref. Church, Brighton Heights, S. I.

FOUNTAIN.

This family is of French origin. James Fontaine, or, de la Fountaine, as it was formerly written, the story of whose escape from France after the Revocation, is given by Smiles; Fontaine, the French fabulist, Sir Andrew Fontaine, the antiquarian, and many others, eminent in science and the arts, are of this family. The progenitor of those of the name in America, was not driven from his native land by the Revocation of the Edict of Nantes in 1685, for there is the notice of a "Charel Fonteyn, a Frenchman, and wife," who came to America in the ship called the "Golden Beaver," in

* Vide App. N. (69.)

1658; there is also a record of Antone Fountain, aged 30, who was a witness in a suit on Staten Island, in 1680. The family is not as numerous in the county as formerly, some branches having become extinct, others having removed from the county. The representative of one branch of the family at the present day, is Mr. Vincent Fountain, of West New Brighton. He is the son of the late Capt. Henry Fountain, who was born 1787, and died May 28th, 1867. He lived for many years in the large house between the Church of the Ascension and the building of the Young Men's Christian Association, on the North Shore. Capt. Henry, and his late brother John, of Tompkinsville, were sons of Vincent Fountain, who was born in 1748, and died Dec. 11, 1819. Vincent was probably the son of Anthony Fountain, who was supervisor in 1767.

Beside the above, there is mention in the county or church records, of the following:

Antone Fontayne, who purchased land in 1686; probably he was the same who was witness in a suit six years before.

Vincent, who both bought and sold land in 1697.

Richard also bought in 1702.

Anthony and Belitze (Isabella) Byvank, his wife, had a daughter baptized May 11, 1729.

Anthony and Annatje Geretson, his wife, had a son Antone, baptized Nov. 3, 1754, a son John, Nov. 20th, 1757, and a son Cornelius, Dec. 23d, 1759. (See foot note.)

Anthony and Susannah, his wife, had a son Charles, baptized Sep. 25th, 1756.

John Fountain and Catharine Fountain were married Dec. 24th, 1804.

Note.—Cornelus Fountain died Jan. 27, 1813, and his wife Elizabeth lived but four days after, having died Jan 31, 1813. They are buried by the side of each other in a field in the town of Southfield, a few rods south of the Old Town road, and east of the S. I. Railroad.

FROST.

The first of this name in this county, as far as can now be ascertained, was Dr. Thomas Frost; he resided at Richmond, and from the fact that courts, supervisors' meetings, and other public bodies met at his house sometimes, we infer that he also kept an inn or tavern. That he was a decided loyalist or tory, is evident from the indictment found against him by the first grand jury which was impanelled after the evacuation of the Island by the British, as may be seen in another place. The first court-house built in the county after the formation of the new government, was upon land purchased from him, which building is still standing, though in a modernized form, and is now owned and occupied by Isaac M. Marsh, Esq. That Dr. Frost was here just before the Revolution, is seen by an entry in the baptismal record of St. Andrew's Church, which records the fact that Thomas and Tamar Frost had a son named William Errell, born February 17th, 1774. They had, at least, three more sons, viz., Samuel, Henry and John; what became of the two last mentioned, we do not positively know, but Samuel continued to reside on the Island; he was twice married, the first time to a lady from New Jersey, the second time to Catharine Bedell, by whom he had one son, the late Samuel H. (see civil list.) Samuel H. married Louisa, daughter of the late Mr. Stephen Ketteltas; their children were Henry (late supervisor of Middletown) and Stephen K.

GARRISON.

Sometimes written GARRETSON, GERAETSON, etc.

There were several of the name emigrated from Holland; the earliest were Gerret Gerretson Van Gelthuys, a tailor—came over, in 1658, in the ship "The Gilded Beaver."

John Gerretson, baker, with his wife and child, came at the same time, and in the same ship.

Wouter and Stoffel came over in February, 1659, in the "Faith." Gerret and Jan came over in December of the same year, in the same ship. There were several others of the name came over in succeeding years.

Whether the family on the Island have all descended from one emigrant, or from more, it is now impossible to determine. The earliest mention of the name on the Island occurs in 1691, when Jacob gave his brother John a power of attorney to sell land on Smoking Point, from which we infer that Jacob was not a resident of the Island, and John was. From 1698 to 1702 we find the names of Frederick, Christopher Lambert, (Sheriff in 1802) and Seger, all as land owners.

Hendrick is mentioned in the County records 1768; he lived on the Clinch property, Richmond Road, near Fingerboard Road; his mouth, it is said, when he closed it, contracted into wrinkles, like that of some kind of fishes; he is said to have been remarkably athletic and active, and his voice was so exceeding powerful, he could make himself heard over a mile. His son Harmanus was born in April, 1732, and died July 3, 1813. Harmanus' son John, (always named as John, Esq.) was born in 1761, and died December 19, 1837; he was County Judge from 1803 to 1823, Presidential elector in 1808, and surrogate 1820. John's son Harmanus was Member of Assembly, 1825; it was humorously said of him that he carried more weight in the Assembly than any other member, for he weighed over 300 pounds. This Harmanus had three brothers, John, Jun., George and Garret;

John, Jun., was Member of Assembly, 1886; his sons are Jacob C., and John of Fresh Kills.

The venerable John C., now living at Garrison's Station, S. I. R. R., was born March 15, 1788; he is the son of John, and his mother was Elizabeth Conner, sister of the late Col. Richard Conner; his grandfather was usually called Hannis, which is an abbreviation of the word Johannes.

In addition to the above, we find in the several Church records mention made of the following:

Jacob, born Sept. ——, 1766, died July 3, 1847; he married Catharine Simonson, Jan. 18, 1789.

John, known as Col., born 1761, died Aug. 15, 1889; he had a daughter bap. Sept. 7, 1787.

Nicholas and Christina Van Woglom, son Abraham bap. Sept. 21, 1744.

Daniel and Mary had the following children:

Charles, born Feb. 11, 1755.

Jacob, born June 18, 1757.

Daniel, bap. Aug. 22, 1762.

Daniel made his will Dec. 21, 1792, proved Dec. 5, 1798, in which he speaks of his wife Mary, and his children Daniel, Jacob, Charles, Catharine Buskirk, and Mary.

Isaac and Maria Christopher, son Christopher bap. Mar. 21, 1781.

John and Susan Lake, married Dec. 28, 1806.

Charles, Sheriff in 1790, and Adrianche, mentioned in the County records in 1768, we find no further traces of.

GUYON.

This is an ancient and honorable French Protestant family. Some of them escaped at an early date from the persecutions in their native country, and came to America; others remained until the Revocation of the Edict of Nantes, when most of them escaped to Holland, but a few remained to face the peril. William de Guyon de Geis fled to Holland, and took service under William of Orange, and lost an arm in that service in Germany; he died in 1740. Several of his descendants held commissions in the English army. Of those who remained in France, an aged pastor was arrested, and, upon being searched, a letter from Claude Brousson, who was a proscribed preacher, was found upon him, and he was forthwith executed, and the house at Nismes in which he was captured was razed to the ground, as a punishment to its owner for giving him shelter. The last Count Guyon was in the Austrian service as late as 1848. There were, probably, two of the family came to New York at an early date— Gregory and Jaques. The former lived at New Rochelle in 1710, and was then 44 years of age, and his wife, Mary, 40. The latter settled on Staten Island, and received a patent from Sir Edmond Andross, dated March 27th, 1675, for about 178 acres of land on Staten Island, at a quit rent of eight bushels of wheat. This patent is still in existence, and the land is still owned and occupied by one of his direct descendants, Mrs. Dr. Ephraim Clark. We find in our County records notices of two law-suits: one, "Jacob Jeyoung against Isaac See, in 1678; the other, Jaques Jeyoung against ffrancis Martinoe, March 6, 1781." As he was the only individual of the name of Guyon,—or Jeyoung, which is nearer the French pronunciation—he was, without doubt, the plaintiff in both suits, the name Jacob being either a clerical error, or an instance of clerical ignorance. He had a son James, born January 5th, 1714. James had a son James, born March 16th, 1746, whose wife's name was Susannah, and they were the parents of the late Maj. James Guyon, father of Mrs. Clark, known in our civil list as James, Jun., who was born December 24th, 1778, and died March 9th, 1846. He was Member of Assembly in 1812-13, and Representative in Congress in 1819-'20. He was married three times: first, to Ann Bedell, mother of Mrs. C.; second, to Ann Perine; and third, to Martha Seguine; the two last were childless.

The present Maj. James Guyon was the son of Harmanus, and his wife, Elizabeth Holmes, married May 2d, 1802. Harmanus—usually called Harry—was Member of Assembly 1819-'20. He was the son of James by his second wife, Margaret Garrison, and half-brother of James, Jr.

In the old church records of St. Andrews, we find the following, which we are unable to place:

John and Elizabeth Butler married January 12th, 1800.

Cornelius and Getty Mersereau married May 16th, 1807.

HATFIELD.

The tradition of the family is that James Hatfield and a brother came from England long before the Revolution; the brother settled in New Jersey, but James on Staten Island. During the war, James was a decided whig, a rare occurence, particularly on Staten Island, and was incarcerated by the British, or tories, somewhere in New Jersey, but was shortly released by the Americans. His sons were James and John D., who was born April 5, 1777, and died December 3d, 1856; he married Mary, daughter of Jacob Van Pelt, and they were the parents of the following children:

John, Moses, (both whom were lost at sea in December,

1830); Maria, wife of Capt. J. W. Barnes, of Port Richmond ; Jacob died in infancy ; Jacob, born March 17, 1817, and still living in Port Richmond.

There is a record of a Benjamin Hatfield, who married Nanne Merrill, January 10th, 1765, and of Susanna Hatfield, who was the wife of Pieter Decker, and had a child baptized as early as 1718. (See the Decker family). Whether these were members of the same family, it is impossible now to determine, unless there is an error in the family tradition.

HAUGHWOUT.

The date of the arrival, and the name of the progenitor of this family, are lost. It was never very numerous, and the notices of it in the county and church records are few. The earliest mention of it is where Egbert Haughwout was sponsor at a baptism Apr. 20, 1709, and where Peter Haughwout sold land in 1708. Egbert had a daughter bap. May 4, 1714, and Peter and Neltje (Cornelia) Bakker his wife, had eight children baptized between 1710 and 1736.

Jan and Elizabeth Hooglaut had a daughter baptized Oct. 16, 1720.

Peter and Aaltje (Alida) Bennett, of Long Island, had the following children :

A daughter Neltje (Cornelia), bap. July 28, 1751.

A son Peter, June 24, 1752.

A son Nicholas, Mar. 12, 1758, and

A son Wynant, Apr. 20, 1760

He owned a large property at the locality now known as Willow Brook, or the Gun Factory, in Northfield. He made his will Dec. 15, 1787, probated Sep. 6, 1792, in which he speaks of his wife Alle (or Altje), his sons Peter, Nicholas and Wynant, and his daughters Alle Webb, deceased, Nelly Cozine, deceased, and his grand-children, the children of his daughter Nelly, and Alettee, Garrett, Peter and Jacobus.

His son Peter was the father of the late Peter N., of Port Richmond. His son Wynant was the father of Simon, grocer, of Graniteville, and his son Nicholas was father of Nicholas, now deceased, who was engaged in the oyster business, and was the first to introduce oysters "on the Canal Street plan"—that is, stewed or otherwise cooked, before which they could only be procured raw.

Egbert and Elenor Garebrantz had a son Daniel, bap. Mar. 8, 1782.

Nicholas had a daughter bap. Aug. 6, 1786.

Wynant had a son Isaac bap. Oct. 28, 1787.

Peter had a son Daniel, bap. June 7, 1788.

HILLYER.

John Hillyer, sometimes written Hilliard, lived on Staten Island in 1698, and married Elizabeth Dey in 1714.

Their children were John, (supervisor in 1767) Elizabeth, Mary, James, William, Nathaniel, Simon and Lawrence.

The present families of the name are descended from the youngest son Lawrence. His son John (sheriff in 1799 and 1819), was born in July, 1763, and died in July, 1848. His wife Elsie Merrill was born in November, 1768, and died in August, 1858. Their children were Lawrence, (sheriff in 1831

and Member of Assembly 1835 and 1837.)   John B. (Member
of Assembly 1878.)

John B. is the father of James A., late of the firm of Pine,
Hillyer & Co., of West New Brighton; and Abraham, of
the firm of Hillyer and Hartley, of New Brighton, beside
several other children.

Other Hillyers are mentioned in the records of St. Andrew's
Church, as follows:

John and Esther his wife had

A daughter, born Sept. 19, 1756.

A son, Nathaniel, born Oct. 2, 1765.

A daughter, born Nov. 14, 1768.

John, Jr., had a son Abraham, born Jan. 20, 1759.

William and Dinah his wife had

A daughter, born Dec. 24, 1748.

A daughter, born Sept. 11, 1756.

John and Mary his wife had

A daughter, born Mar. 29, 1774.

A son John, born April 18, 1776.

Lawrence and Ann Larzalere married Dec. 4, 1808.

HOLMES.

The progenitor of this family was Obadiah, or, as he sometimes wrote it, "o Badiah;" he came from England in the
latter half of the seventeenth century, and obtained a patent
for a valuable tract of land in Southfield, which remained in
the family for several generations. His name is found in the
county records as early as 1688. There is a link missing in
the family chain, which it now appears to be impossible to

supply; there is no record of the names of his children. His grandson Samuel lived and died on the paternal estate, and had six daughters and two· sons, Baker and Samuel. The latter married Margaret, daughter of Stephen Cole, and had the following children : Samuel, James, John, Cornelius, Van Renselaer, George W. Eliza, and Ann wife of David Mersereau, of Northfield. Several of these are still living.

HOUSMAN.

We have no means of ascertaining when the first of this name came to America from Holland. The earliest mention of the name is found in the assessment roll of Boswyck (Bushwick) L. I., where the name of Charles Housman occurs in the years 1675 and 1676. The earliest mention of the name in a church record on Staten Island is as follows:

John and Wynje Symons (Simonson) had

A daughter, bap. Sept. 4, 1726.

A son Aart (Aaron or Arthur) May 24, 1730.

A daughter ——, June 1, 1732.

A son Dirk, Feb. 29, 1736, died July 29, 1807.

A son Abraham, Dec. 9, 1739.

A daughter Elizabeth, Oct. 11, 1743, and

A daughter Jemima, July 19, 1748.

Isaac, born Nov. 4, 1775, died Dec. 2, 1857; he was married to Hannah Perine Apr. 9, 1807.

Peter had a daughter bap. Aug. 6, 1785, and another Dec. 7, 1788.

The most prominent members of the family were John, who was many years one of the inferior Judges of the Common Pleas, Member of Assembly 1804, Surrogate 1809, and Supervisor repeatedly.

Isaac R. was also one of the Judges, Member of Assembly, 1823, and Supervisor repeatedly. The Sailors' Snug Harbor property was purchased from him.

Notices of the family are extremely meagre in our county records.

James made his will Nov. 1, 1801, proved Sep. 22, 1808, in which he speaks only of his brothers Anthony and Jacob.

JACOBSON.

This was a Danish family. The first of the name found in our records, is Christian, who is mentioned in the article on the Moravian Church. His son, John Van Deventer, was born in 1768, and died in 1826. He had the following sons: Peter, dec.; Cornelius, living on Long Island—he married a daughter of Isaac R. Housman, Esq.; Bedell, dec.; Israel, dec.; Abraham, dec.

JOHNSON.

It is impossible to trace the Johnson's back to their several progenitors in this county. Evidently they are not of the same origin; the name is English, but some of them are of Dutch extraction, having Anglicised the Dutch name of Jansen. We give extracts from the various records indiscriminately, leaving each one of the name to appropriate his own ancestors. The earliest is:

Peter, who was plaintiff in a law suit in 1680.

Thomas and Ann Bouwman, son Casper, bap. June 30, 1728.

Johannes and Jannetje (Jane) Glascow, son Thomas, bap. Feb. 29, 1736.

Nathaniel and Sophia Van Gelder, son Henricks, bap. Nov. 19, 1738.

Niers and Sara Morgen had daughters bap. 1731, 1739 and 1740.

Peter and Mary Taylor, married Oct. 24, 1754.

Isaac and Elender Bowman married ———, 1764.

Peter and Malli (Molly) Lister, son Jouneton (Jonathan) bap. Oct. 2, 1755.

John and Cornelia Ceilo, son Peter, bap. Nov. 7, 1758.

The above are from the Dutch Church records, except the marriages of Isaac and Peter, which with the following are from St. Andrews.

Dowe and Margaret, daughter Ann, born May 7, 1771.

Dowe made his will Nov. 10, 1783, proved June 7, 1784, in which he mentions his sons Dowe and James.

Winant and Mary had daughter Sophia, born Dec. 17, 1772, and son David born Apr. 13, 1774.

Winant, not the above, made his will June 18, 1803, proved June 30, 1803, in which he mentions his wife Mary and sons Winant and Jesse; these sons married—Winant, Catharine Guyon, Nov. 26, 1797, and Jesse, Rachel Totten Jan. 11, 1804.

Mattice (Matthias) had a son William, born July 17, 1751, who was baptized May —, 1772, then an adult.

George had a son Thomas, born Aug. 17, 1771.

Isaac and Ploney (Appolonia) Frome, married Mar. —, 1772.

Nathaniel and Catharine Woglom, married Nov. 9, 1791.

Lewis and Phebe Van Pelt, married Dec. 24, 1793.

John born ——, 1770, died June 2d, 1832, and Patty (Martha) Bedell, married Mar. 23, 1794.

He was a potter, and carried on his business on the Shore Road, in the vicinity of Elm Park, Port Richmond; they had the following sons:

John, merchant at Richmond, S. I., born Jan. 3, 1795, died Dec. 19, 1859.

Joseph B., merchant at Port Richmond, born Nov. —, 1796, died July 4, 1849.

Israel D., merchant at Port Richmond, born Apr. 15, 1808, died Feb. 9, 1873; and James.

Jacob, brother of the potter, married Eliza Haughwout, July 28, 1795; their sons were Peter H., James, Isaac, Benjamin and Jacob.

William, brother of the potter, married Catharine Martling, Apr. 28, 1802; their sons were John, James, William, Edward and Channing: they had also a daughter Sarah, who married Hugh Gibson, and died Aug. 25th, 1826, in her 69th year; their son John, born Feb. 13, 1803, died Nov. 3, 1865.

Edward, brother of the potter, born Oct. 12, 1776, died Sep. 4, 1856.

Abraham and Jane Jennings, married Sep. 24, 1794.

David and Jane Winant, married June 23, 1796.

Ephraim and Catharine Laforge, married Oct. 10, 1797.

James and Letitia Totten, married Feb. 20, 1805.

Anthony and Fanny Oakley, married Jan. 28, 1807.

Esek, of Tottenville, was grandson of James, and son of Abraham, who built one of the first houses on the Billop estate, after the sale by confiscation.

JONES.

There were several families of this very common name in the county, from early dates, between whom there appears to have been no relationship whatever.

We submit a brief genealogy of some of the early families of this name.

The earliest one named is Edward, whose wife was Catharine Decker, and they had the following children:

Edward bap. July 20, 1718, died young.

Mattheus, bap. Nov. 2, 1719.

Abigail, bap. April 22, 1722.

Edward, bap. Aug. 14, 1726.

Mattheus, above named, married Margaritje (Margaret) Gowan, and they had a daughter Catharine, baptized June 7, 1743.

There was a John whose wife was Rachael Van Engelen, and they had the following children:

Elizabeth, bap. April 10, 1732.

Johannes, bap. March 9, 1735.

A daughter, bap. —— —, 1737.

Lucretia, bap. March 30, 1740.

Isaac, bap. April 22, 1747.

Abraham and Jannetje Persnet had a daughter Jane, bap. May 2, 1758.

Edward and Martha, his wife, had a son Abraham, born March 31, 1772.

JOURNEAY.

Moillart Journeay, from Pays de Vaud, came to America in April, 1663, in the ship called "The Spotted Cow," but where he settled is not known. The earliest mention of the family in connection with the Island, is in the county records, where John Journeay bought and sold land in 1700. The name is not again met with in any church record now in existence, until we find it in that of St. Andrew's Church, about the middle of the last century, as follows:

John and Martha his wife had the following children:

John, born Jan. 4, 1752.
Albert, born Mar. 8, 1755.
Nicholas, born Aug. 22, 1756.
William, born Aug. 6, 1759, and
Richard, born Aug. 7, 1771.

The above named Nicholas is mentioned in the county records in 1791 as Nicholas, Jun.; there must therefore have been another Nicholas, whose name we have nowhere met.

Nicholas, son of John, had a son Nicholas, bap. Nov. 1, 1789.

Joseph and Mary Winant were married Dec. 29, 1807.

John and Patience Cole were married July —, 1802.

John (not the last named, unless Patience Cole was his 2d wife) made his will Mar. 7, 1803, proved Apr. 21, 1803, in which he speaks of his wife Patience, his sons Albert, Robert, Abraham, John, William, James and Richard, and his daughters Martha Randolph, Catharine Fountain and Mary, wife of Dr. Henderson.

LAFORGE.

The name of ——— De la Forge appears in the assessment roll of Boswyck (Bushwick) in 1676, and among those who took the oath of allegiance in Kings County in 1687, is the name of Adrian La fforge, who had then been in the County fifteen years. In 1738 there was an Adrian Laforge, who bought land on Staten Island. From the similarity of the name, the inference is natural that if they are not identical, they were connected ; this is, however, conjecture. There appears to have been two branches of the family, the Castleton and the Westfield, who may or may not have had a common origin. The paucity of notices in the old records of the County and churches, and the absence of family records, renders it impossible to trace the family far. The present living representative of the Castleton branch is Mr. G. M. Laforge, of Illinois; the late Mr. Peter D. Laforge, also of Illinois, and the late Capt. John Laforge, of West New Brighton, were his brothers ; their father was David, and their mother Gertrude, daughter of John Martling, (see Martling family); David's father was Peter, who was the son of Benjamin ; David's brothers were Peter, John, Benjamin, Jacob, Richard Channing Moore ; Peter, David's brother was the father of Mr. Peter C. and David of Port Richmond.

Of the Westfield branch, we have only the following notices :

David and Catharine had a son Henry Seguine, bap. May 15, 1790.

John and Phebe Bedell married Sept. 15, 1804.

James and Catharine Winant married Feb. 8, 1806.

David and Ann Johnson married July 8, 1807.

LAKE.

This family is probably of English origin. The first mention of the name occurs in the county records, where the name of Daniel is recorded as having purchased land in 1696 and 1699. Daniel, probably, had several sons, among whom were Joseph, Abraham, and Thomas. Joseph had a son Joseph, baptized April 20, 1708, who married Aaltye (Alida) Burbank, and had a son Abraham, baptized March 26, 1731.

Joseph had also another son Abraham, baptized 1715.

Abraham (Daniel's son) also had a son Joseph, baptized 1708, and Abraham, 1715.

Thomas, perhaps the youngest of Daniel's sons, married Jannetje (Jane) Stryker, and had a son Thomas, baptized October 19, 1718.

Here occurs a gap which we are unable to fill.

Joseph, born July 8th, 1753, and his wife, Catharine, born June 2, 1755, both died March 14, 1813, within one hour of each other. They had a daughter Patience, born May 30, 1790.

There was another Joseph also born 1753, and died May 24, 1843, in his 90th year.

There was still another Joseph, born in 1773, and died March 16, 1854. He lived on the Manor Road near the Four Corners, Castleton.

William and Mary Tysen, his wife, had the following sons:

    William, born November 16, 1769.

    Bornt, born March 25, 1771 ; killed October 27, 1815.

    Joseph, born May 12, 1777.

Bornt had the following sons: William, Joseph, Daniel, and John, of whom John is still living (1876) at Graniteville.

There was a Daniel W. born 1780, died October 6, 1835.

Daniel and Margaret, his wife, had a son Daniel, born May 12, 1777.

Cornelius and Susan Androvet were married April 6, 1794.

Joseph and Eliza Van Pelt were married January 20, 1798.

Daniel and Margaret Jackson were married June 5, 1802.

Daniel Lake made his will October 13, 1789, proved September 4, 1792, in which he mentions his wife Sarah, his sons Daniel and Joseph, and his grandson Daniel, son of his son William, deceased.

LARZELERE.

The earliest mention of this name occurs in the county records, where Jacob bought land in 1686. Nicholas bought land in 1693; he was at one time sheriff of the county. There was another Jacob, probably a son of Nicholas, whose wife's name was Alice; they had a son Daniel, born June 16, 1757, and a son Benjamin, born Oct. 22, 1761.

Nicholas, probably a brother of Jacob, whose wife's name was Sarah; they had a daughter Johanna, born Jan. 7, 1768.

Jacob and Elsy, (or Alice, the same mentioned above,) had a son Richard, born June 18, 1771.

Benjamin, (not the one mentioned above) was born July 6, 1740, and died Oct. 6, 1802; he made his will June 17, 1802, in which he mentions his wife Sarah, and his children Benjamin, Jacob and Catharine.

The family, once an important one in the county, is now nearly, if not quite, extinct, and it is impossible to obtain a connected genealogy.

There was a Rev. Jacob, a minister of the Ref. Dutch Church in N. and S. Hampton, Penn., from 1797 to 1819, who was probably connected with the Staten Island family.

LATOURETTE.

The original Latourette was a French Huguenot, but when he came to America is unknown. The family is not among the earliest settlers on Staten Island. The first mention of the name we have found is as follows:

Jean and Maria Mersereau had the following children:

A son David, bap. Apr. 24, 1726, David Latourette sponsor.

A son Anthony, Jan. 24, 1730.

A son Henry, Jan. 24, 1731.

Pierre La Turrete and Mariamne Mersereaux had

A son Daniel, bap. Mar. 3, 1728.

Twin sons David and Jacques, Oct. 31, 1730.

David and Catharine Poillon, son Jaques, bap. Mar. 19, 1732.

James, probably one of the Jaques mentioned above, and Elizabeth his wife, had a son John born Dec. 11, 1764.

A son Jonathan, born Jan. 31, 1766, and

A son Henry, born Apr. 22, 1775.

David and Elizabeth his wife had a daughter Catharine, born Nov. 9, 1766.

John and Susannah his wife had a son John, born Sep. 30, 1764.

James and Mary his wife had a son David, born July 7, 1786.

David and Phebe Cole married Nov. 12, 1806.

Henry of Fresh Kills, weaver, made his will. Jan 19, 1794, proved Dec. 30, 1794, in which he speaks of his wife Sarah, his brother Henry, dec'd, his sons Henry, John and Peter, and his daughters Susan, wife of Peter Cole, and Ann, wife of William de Groot.

Peter's wife was Elizabeth Androvette.

ANNALS OF STATEN ISLAND.

LISK.

This family was never very numerous on the Island, and we find little mention of it in any records.

James, the earliest mentioned, had a son John bap. Mar. 25, 1701. He is also mentioned as having bought land in 1706; he had a son Thomas, who married Catalyntje Van Pelt, and had daughters baptized in 1729, 1731, 1739 and 1745; John, son of James, married Rachel Haughwout, and had a son Jacob bap. Jan. 2, 1728.

Matthias and Anastasia had a son Moses born Dec. 7, 1766.

John and Mary had a son Thomas born Sep. 19, 1756; he made his will Aug. 24, 1793, proved Nov. 4, 1793, in which he mentions his children Thomas, Franky and Catharine.

There is an Alexander Lisk mentioned in the Court Records in 1734.

LOCKMAN.

LOOKERMAN, LAKEMAN, LACKMAN, LOOKERMAN, &c.

This is one of the oldest of the Dutch families in the province. The first mention of the name is that of Govert Lockermans, (sometimes spelled Lookermans), who arrived in America in 1633, in the carvel St. Martyn. He was a minor when he arrived, and came as an apprentice, but was immediately taken into the service of the Company. He soon contrived to make himself conspicuous, especially in leading attacks upon the Indians, on Staten Island and elsewhere.

The earliest mention of the name in the records, occurs in

1680, when Abraham Lakeman* is said to have owned a parcel of woodland on the south of the Fresh-kill. About this
time there were several of the name on the Island—Abraham,
mentioned above, whose name is found again on the records,
in 1684 and 1692; Lewis, who was defendant in a suit July
6, 1681; and Peter, who sold land in 1684. These three probably were brothers. There was an Isaac, perhaps a son of
one of the above, of whom we only know that his wife was
Catharine Christopher, and that they had a son Lewis, bap.
May 23, 1731.

Abraham, and Elizabeth his wife, had two daughters born
—Sarah, in 1762, and Margaret in 1767, and a son Abraham,
born Apr. 4, 1772.

Isaac, and his wife Martha, had the following sons:

David, born Jan. 26, 1768; Jacob, born July 21, 1771, and
Joseph, born Oct. 7, 1775.

William and Mary his wife had a daughter Sarah, born
Oct. 4, 1772.

Isaac and Margaret his wife had a son William, born
Nov. 24, 1772.

There was another Isaac, born 1758, and died May 1, 1814.

Samuel and Catharine Crowal, were married Mar. 16, 1790.

Nathaniel made his will Dec. 12, 1795, proved May 24, 1808,
in which he mentions his wife Martha, his daughter Susanna,
and his sons Isaac and John.

This family is also gradually dying out.

* Vide App N. (70.)

MANEE.

Originally written Manes. This is a Westfield family concerning which the notices, in either county or church records, are exceedingly meagre. We have found but few shreds of its history.

Peter, and Mary Brooks his wife, had a daughter baptized August 8, 1726.

Abraham and Anna Jansen, his wife, had a son Abraham, baptized May 26, 1728.

Abraham and Sarah du Chesne, had a daughter Sarah, baptized March 30, 1740.

Abraham had a son Isaac, baptized May 15, 1790.

Peter and Mary Pryor were married Jan. 4, 1804.

William and Eliza Pryor were married April ——, 1808.

Abraham and Mary Woglom were married Oct. 8, 1808.

Isaac made his will May 14, 1794, proved July 18, 1794, in which he speaks of his brothers Abraham and Peter, and sister Hannah Prior. His will is dated on the day of his death, at which time he was 46 years old.

MARTLING.

This name is not met with at a very early date; when its connection with the Island began, is unknown; the earliest mention of the family in our local records, is in 1724, when Isaac Martling and Anna Van Name his wife, had a daughter bap. Jan. 10; a son John, Jan. 21, 1731, a Barent Martling being present as a sponsor. He died in infancy.

Peter and Jannetje (Jane) Heereman had a son John, bap. Apr. 26, 1748.

Barent and Susanna Gerretson had a son Barent bap. Sep. 19, 1749, and Barent, Sen., was sponsor. There were three generations present on this occasion, represented by three Barent Martlings.

Peter (same as above) had a son Benjamin, bap. Sept. 17, 1752, and another son Johannes or John Oct. 11, 1743.

Barent, son of Barent above named, married Nannie Tuson (Tyson), and had a son Barent, born Jan. 10, 1776.

Johannes or John, son of Peter, was the grandfather of Mr. Peter L. Martling, now (1876) residing near the Four Corners ; he made his will Dec. 15, 1798, which was proved Jan. 8, 1802 ; he speaks of six daughters and two sons, viz.: Annatje (Anna), Elizabeth, Catharine (married William Johnson, died Nov. 19, 1852, in her 72d year), Gitty (Gertrude), married first David Laforge, second John Laforge, Jane, Catharine, and Clarissa (died unmarried Aug. 15, 1872, aged 81 years), and Garret and John. The former owned the property now belonging to A. C. Bradley, Esq.; the latter owned the farm now occupied by his son Peter L.; he married Dorcas Laforge Jan. 3, 1802.

Benjamin and Aala (Alida) Cozine were married June 18, 1795.

MARTINO.

Gaston Martineau, a surgeon of Dieppe, settled in England in 1685, and was a French refugee. He had several sons, whose descendants still reside in England, and many of them are distinguished. The family in America is a collateral branch, and were in this country and on the Island before Gaston left France. We find the name of Francis in our county records as defendant in a suit with Jaques Jeyoung in 1681, and as selling land in 1691.

Stephen was born 1727, and died May 9, 1801; he owned and resided on the property now known as the Poor House Farm. He was one of the corporators of the Moravian Church.

Benjamin, brother of Stephen, was born 1742, and died May 17, 1824.

Benjamin, son of above was born Apr. 4, 1766, and died Nov. 20, 1814. He was father of Mr. Gabriel Martino, residing near Four Corners, Castleton.

Stephen was father of Mr. Gabriel Martino, residing between Graniteville and Bull's Head.

MERRILL.

This family have descended from Richard Merrill and Sarah Wells his wife, natives of Warwickshire, England, who emigrated to America about the year 1675, and settled on Staten Island. As their family was the only one of the name on the Island, they had among their children the following sons: William, Richard, Thomas, Philip and Philys, unless the two last names are identical, and perhaps John, for we find in the Albany records the name of William as owning land on Staten Island in 1688; Philys bought land of Richard (father or brother?) in 1711.

Richard married Elsie Dorlant, and had the following children:

Richard, bap. Sep. 22, 1709, who died young.

Elsie, bap. Apr. 1, 1708, by Dom. Freeman.

Richard, bap. 1715.

Lambert, bap. Jan. 1, 1721.

Susanna, bap. Sep. 13, 1724.

Philip and Elizabeth Bakker, (Baker) his wife, had the following children:

Catherine and Susanna, twins, bap. July 4, 1725.

Philip, bap. Feb. 24, 1727.

Nicholas, bap. Nov. 24, 1728.

Elisabet, bap. Apr. 8, 1733.

Neeltje (Cornelia) bap. Mar. 9, 1735.

Thomas and Jenne Gewan had a son Richard—no date of baptism.

John and Gertrude Simonson had a daughter, bap. Sep. 18, 1726.

William; of his descendants we have no account.

The above are the children and grand-children of the orig-inal pair, so far as the church records throw any light upon the matter.

Richard, son of Thomas, had the following children:

Margaretta, bap. Jan. 1, 1738.

Annatje, (Anna) bap. Apr. 19, 1743; no others mentioned.

Jan and Aeltje (Alida) Bennet had a son Simon, and a daughter bap. on the same day, May 6, 1745.

Thomas and Eva Jones had a daughter bap. Oct. 31, 1756. This Thomas made his will Dec. 31, 1791, proved Apr. 30, 1808, in which he mentions his wife Eva and his sons John, Thomas and Matthew.

John, son of Thomas and Eva (known in the family as Bon-nis) was born 1742, and died Dec. 19, 1826. His wife's name was Charity.

Thomas (known as " Sawmill Thomas,") son of John and Eva, had a son John, bap. Aug. 17, 1788.

There was a John, Jun., who had a daughter bap. Nov. 7,

1790, and John Y., who was born in 1770, and died June 6, 1858, but they are probably distinct persons; John, Jun., more probably was the son of Joseph and Martha, and was born Apr. 4, 1765.

Joseph also had a daughter Mary, born Jan. 16, 1763.

John and Ann his wife had a daughter bap. Nov. 7, 1758.

Lambert, (son of Richard and Elsie), and Tabitha, had a son Richard, born July 9, 1765; a son Jonathan born May 24, 1774; a daughter Tabitha, born Feb. 18, 1770, who married Capt. John W. Blake, and died Jan. 12, 1861, aged nearly 91 years; also a daughter Elsie, born 1768, married John Hillyer 1785, and was the mother of Hon. Lawrence Hillyer, dec., and Hon. John B. Hillyer, still living (1876) at New Springville.

William and Ann Merrill were married Aug. —, 1776.

Abraham and Ann Merrill were married Oct. 3d, 1790.

Mary, widow of —— Merrill, made her will Jan. 10, 1789, proved Nov. 30, 1789; reference has been made to this will before, and the bequest made to her daughter Mary, the wife of Nathaniel Robbins.

The family was once numerous, and have largely intermarried with other families of the Island. The property belonging to them in Northfield was extensive, and a part of it is still in the possession of some of them.

The public road known as Lambert's Lane, leading to Watchogue, was named from Lambert Merrill, mentioned above.

MERSEREAU.

[From Family Records and Traditions.]

John Mersereau was a native of France, and a Protestant. In his youth he was possessed of extraordinary physical strength. He studied law, but disliking the confinement of study, he learned the trade of a saddler, which he subsequently carried on extensively. He was also captain of a military company, armed with pikes, the members of which attained great skill in the use of that weapon.. When he went abroad, he always wore a sword at his side. One evening he met three men habited as friars, whom he saluted, saying "Good evening, gentlemen." They immediately charged him with being a Protestant—otherwise he would have said "Good evening, fathers." He replied, "I know but one Father, who is in Heaven." They then drew their sabres, which were concealed under their cloaks, and attacked him, and he was obliged to defend himself; the result was, he killed one, wounded another, and the third fled. For some unexplained reason, he was never molested for this deed. He died young, and left three sons—Joshua, Paul and Daniel—and two daughters, Mary and Martha. These children, with their mother, fled from France to England 1685, immediately after the Revocation; but James II, having just ascended the throne, and being a Roman Catholic, they feared further persecution, and all, with the exception of Paul, who remained and followed his father's business, continued their flight to America. They had intended to settle at Philadelphia, but they were driven to New York by stress of weather. They settled on Staten Island, where their mother died, and was buried in the French church-yard (on the Seaman farm, Westfield).

Daniel was a tailor; Joshua married a Latourette, and died May 23, 1756, aged over 93 years. They had a son Joshua, who was born May 18, 1696, and died July 9, 1769; his wife was Maria Corsen (sometimes written Mary), daughter of Jacob Corsen; she was born Oct. 24, 1704, and died July 3, 1768. Their children were:

*Joshua, born Sep. 26, 1728, died June 10, 1804.
†Jacob, born Apr. 23, 1730, died Sep. 7, 1804.
John, born Mar. 2, 1732, died ———.
Elizabeth, born Jan. 4, 1734, died in infancy.
David, born Nov. 10, 1735, died July 19, 1768.
Mary, born Jan. 14, 1738, died ———.
Cornelius, born July 27, 1739, died July 27, 1814.
Paul, born Feb. 23, 1741, died Jan. 26, 1828.
Elizabeth, born Nov. 26, 1742, died ———.
Rachel, born Feb. 27, 1746, died July 9, 1769.

Paul, son of Joshua and Maria Corsen, married Elizabeth Barnes, born Apr. 21, 1751, died May 26, 1838, their children were:

Joshua, born Feb. 7, 1773, died Mar. 7, 1847.
Nancy, born Apr. 4, 1775, died Nov. 30, 1851.
Mary, born Feb. 2, 1777, died June 6, 1858.
Elizabeth, born June 20, 1779, died May 8, 1855.
Rachel, born June 30, 1781, died Feb. 23, 1863.
‡Paul, born Mar. 14, 1784, died July 21, 1856.
Margaret, born Mar. 27, 1787.
Gertrude, born Nov. 30, 1789.

Joshua, son of Paul and Elizabeth, married Deborah Brit-

* He was repeatedly Member of Assembly between 1777 and 1786.

† Jacob made his will July 16, 1804, proved Sept. 18, 1804, in which he speaks of his wife Charity, and his children John, and Mary, wife of Thomas Cubberly; Elizabeth, wife of Daniel De Hart; Sophia, wife of John Crocheron; Jacob, David, and Peter. He was the Col. Jacob Mersereau, whose escape from the British during the Revolution is alluded to elsewhere. His son Jacob was the father of John T. and Alfred Mersereau, of Graniteville, and Member of Assembly 1832 and 1838. His son Peter, still living on the old homestead, born in 1788, was Member of Assembly 1845. Col. Jacob had also a son John by his first marriage, who married a Cruser, and lived in an old stone house, on the turn of the road west of the Snug Harbor, and was father-in-law to the late Judge Abraham Crocheron.

‡ Paul was Member of Assembly 1834, and for several years subsequently a Judge of the Court of Common Pleas.

ton, Jan. 7, 1801.   She was born Aug. 4, 1782, and died
Mar. 26, 1840 ; their children were :

    Nathaniel, born Oct. 18, 1802, died in infancy,
    Paul, born Sept. 20, 1804.
    Mary, born Jan. 29, 1807.
    ———— twins, born Jan. 19, 1810.
    Cornelius, born May 12, 1811.
    * Joshua, born Jan. 28, 1814.
    Elsey, born Aug. 30, 1817, dec'd.
    Elizabeth, born May, 5, 1820, dec'd.
    Debora, born Apr. 7, 1823.
    John, born May 28, 1826, died in infancy.
    Margaret.

Thus far we have traced but one branch of the family ;
what notices we have found in the public records, of other
branches, we give indiscriminately.

There was a John mentioned in the County records in 1730 ;
he was probably the same with Jean, whose wife's name was
Craage ; they had a son Joshua baptised Feb., 1731, and subsequently a son Daniel.   This Daniel married Cornelia Vanderbilt, and had a son John, baptized Mar. 4, 1759.

Etienne (Stephen) and Ann Mitchell had a son Daniel
baptized, no date ; a daughter Jan. 1, 1735, and a son Richard, May, 1740.

There was a Joshua had a son Harmanus baptized June 8,
1788.

There was a Paul here as early as 1728, sponsor at a
baptism.

Peter and Rebecca his wife had the following children :
    Sarah, born Mar. 28, 1769.
    Daniel, born Aug. 27, 1771, died July 16, 1855.
    John, bap. Nov., 1775.
Peter died June 16, 1808, born 1734.   See *Note.*

There was a John born Dec., 1737, died July 30, 1811.

John and Charity had a son John born Apr. 13, 1757 ; son
Lawrence Mar. 28, 1761.

* Joshua was Member of Assembly 1857, and County Clerk from 1843 to 1852.

Paul and Frances had a son John born May 2, 1759.

Stephen and Lydia had the following children:

Sarah, born Sep. 8. 1766.

Daniel, born Dec. 6, 1768.

Stephen, born Feb. 14, 1774.

Joshua and Mary had the following children:

Stephen, born May 5, 1770.

Joshua, bap. Sept. 6, 1772.

Daniel and Susan had a daughter Ann bap. July 6, 1789.

Daniel and Ann had a daughter Cornelia bap. June 26, 1791.

Henry and Eliza Laforge married Sept. 6, 1790.

Jacob and Mary Crocheron married Sept. 5, 1798.

Daniel and Alida Lake married Oct. 6, 1798.

Daniel and Eliza Winant married Feb. 8, 1800.

Stephen and Lanah (Helen) Winant married Nov. 21, 1802.

John and Ann Parlee married Dec. 31, 1808.

Joshua and Susannah Story married Dec. 10, 1805.

There were others of this name who emigrated from Holland, but where they settled is not known. Dunlap says, "The Hugnenots who fled to Holland after the bloody and complicated treachery and murder performed by the papists under Charles IX, had remained among their Dutch brethren until many of their descendants had become, in language and manners, assimilated to the Hollanders, and emigrated to this country more Dutch than French; such as the Duryeas, Cortelyous, Mersereaus, and many others."

Note.—Peter Mersereau made his will May 6, 1800, proved July 25, 1808, in which he alludes to his wife without naming her, and mentions his children Elizabeth, Rebecca, Catharine, Ann, Sarah, Daniel and William.

There is another branch of the family, not located on Staten Island, of which Capt. Lawrence Mersereau, who was born Jan. 4, 1773, and died at Union, Broome County, N. Y., January 24, 1873. At the age of 25 he married Hannah Christopher, and had the following children: Hester, Maria, Joshua, Clarissa, George W. Lawrence, Mary, William,

Hannah and John C. Capt. Lawrence's father's name was Joshua.

METCALFE.

Though not among the old, this family is among the most prominent ones of the county. Simon, the progenitor of the family on Staten Island, came from England in 1765, and settled in New York city, and was subsequently appointed deputy surveyor of the colony. He left his son George in England to be educated until he was seventeen years of age, when he joined his father in this country. After studying law, he resided at Albany for a time, then went to Johnstown, Fulton county, N. Y. He married the daughter of Commodore Silas Talbot. In 1796 Gov. John Jay appointed him Assistant Attorney-General, which office he held until 1811. He then removed to New York, where he practiced law until 1816, when he removed to Staten Island, and in 1818, when the office of District Attorney was made a county office, he was appointed to perform its duties. He died in 1826. His children were Maria, who married William S. Root, of Tompkinsville; Silas Talbot; Simon; Catharine, who was the first wife of John R. Simonson; Henry Bleecker; Georgiana, who married Daniel Fenn, of Massachusetts; Louisa, twins, and George.

Henry Bleecker was born January 20th, 1805, studied law with his father, and admitted to the bar in 1826. The same year he was appointed District Attorney for Richmond county, which office he held until 1833. In 1840 he was appointed a County Judge, and the same year U. S. Boarding Officer at Quarantine, in the Revenue Department, which place he occupied until 1843.   In 1847 he was elected County Judge and Surrogate, the two officers having been united, and re-elected from time to time until near the close of 1875, at the end of which year he would have been legally disqualified by age, but he resigned to take his seat as Member of Congress, to which he had been elected, and he is now, 1876, performing the duties of that office as Representative of the 1st Congressional District of the State of New York, in the 1st Session of the 44th Congress.

MORGAN.

This family was on Staten Island at an early date, but the notices of them in the records are very few. Thomas Morgan was a member of the Colonial Assembly from this county in 1692, &c. This is the first occurrence of the name in the county records. His name occurs again in the Dutch Church records as having a son Abraham, baptized May 5, 1696, and a daughter Martha, September 7, 1698.

Thomas, (probably a son of the former,) and Magdalena Staats his wife, had the following children:

A daughter Elisabet, baptized Feb. 7, 1725.

A daughter Magdalena, bap. Feb. 12, 1727.

A son Pieter, bap. March 9, 1729.

A son Thomas, bap. Oct. 10, 1731, and

A daughter Sarah, bap. Sept. 16, 1739.

The name does not again appear until 1754, December 16, when William Morgan and Elizabeth Winter were married.

It is probable that William was the son of Pieter mentioned above, though not certain. William had a son John, who lived and died in the vicinity of New Springville. Among his children was a son Charles who married a Vroom, and they were the parents of Mr. Henry C., of Travisville, and his brother, the late John, of Mariner's Harbor.

PERINE.

The original orthography of the name was Perrin. Count Perrin was a Huguenot refugee from Nouere; the American family are not descended from him, but the original emigrant was akin to him. The first occurrence of the name in this county was in 1687, where Daniel Perine sold land, and he was probably the progenitor of the Perines of the present day. Like many other old families in the county, they have a family record, but very imperfect, except perhaps for the last two or three generations. The branch which we are able to trace, lived for a century and a half, or more, in the same house, which is still standing, and occupied by them, on the Richmond road, a short distance north of Garrison's Station, on the Staten Island Railroad. It is probably the oldest dwelling house in the county occupied by the family who built it.

Cornelius S. and Joseph E., still residing in the old house, are the sons of Simon S., who was the son of

Joseph, born June 4, 1759, died April 16th, 1814. Joseph's brothers were Edward, born July 6, 1766, and Henry, born Nov. 29, 1768, and married Mary Winant June 21, 1795;

they were the parents of Mrs. Elizabeth, relict of the late Richard Tysen, Esq.

Joseph's parents were Edward and Ann; Edward died during the Revolution.

We are unable to trace the pedigree of any branch of the family beyond Edward, with any degree of certainty. Probably Edward was the son, possibly the grandson, of Daniel, whom we suppose to be the original.

In addition to the above, the following are found on the county and church records, on tomb-stones, etc.

Henry and Susannah his wife had a son Edward, born Feb. 19, 1758; a son Peter, born May 22d, 1764; Henry made his will Apr. 10, 1788, which was proved June 7, 1788, in which he mentions his wife Susannah and his children David and Cornelius, then minors, and his other children, Edward, Margaret, and Susannah, Abraham, Henry, Nancy and Mary. This younger Henry was a weaver, and made his will Oct. 29, 1792, which was proved April 2, 1793, in which he speaks of his brothers David, Cornelius and Edward, but alludes to no wife nor children.

Henry and Ann his wife had a son Abraham, born Feb. 1, 1766.

Henry and Hannah his wife had a son Henry, born June 5, 1767.

James and Nannie his wife had a daughter Sophia, born July 17, 1767.

William and Miranda his wife had a son Peter, baptized June 27, 1790.

Edward and Patience Mersereau were married June 7, 1790, and had a daughter Mary, born Oct. 9, 1790.

Abraham and Sarah Rezeau were married Aug. 24, 1790, and had a son Peter Rezeau, born Sep. 20, 1791.

Peter and Mary Bedell were married Dec. 31, 1788.

Edward and Adriar Guyon were married Jan. 20, 1791.

Henry and Magdalena Simonson were married June, 19, 1800.

Cornelius and Mary McLean were married Mar. 31, 1804.

Edward, born in 1745, died Nov. 22, 1818.

James G., born Aug. 29, 1796, died Sep. 17, 1833.

There was a Peter, living in 1766, and a Henry in 1767, who were interested in the purchase or sale of land.

————

POILLON.

The first mention of the name we have found, was in connection with Staten Island, when Jaques Poullian was appointed a Justice for Richmond County, Dec. 14, 1689, by Leisler. The family was never numerous, and the notices of them in the local records are few.

Jaques is frequently mentioned as buying or selling land prior to 1703. After him we have no notice of any member of the family for half a century; then John, and Margaret his wife, had a son John, born June 6, 1758.

A son Peter, born Jan. 27, 1768, and

A son James, bap. Nov. 3, 1772.

James and Frances his wife had a son John bap. Nov. 14, 1762.

Peter and Margaret his wife had a son John, born Oct. 28, 1770.

A son Peter, born Mar. 6, 1772; this Peter was a communicant in St. Andrew's Church, 1792, after his father's death. (See history of that church.)

Abraham and Susan Cole married June 17, 1790; he died young.

John and Elizabeth Seguine married July 5, 1792.

Abraham made his will July 20, 1791, proved Aug. 8,

1791, in which he mentions his wife Susan and his son Peter, a minor.

John, named above, made his will Mar. 16, 1802, proved Feb. 18, 1808; mentions his wife Margaret, his daughters Mary, Margaret, Ann, Sarah and Catharine, and his sons Peter, John and James, deceased.

POST.

Adrian Post, who was, without doubt, the progenitor of the family on Staten Island, was commander of a ship which brought emigrants to the colony before 1650. He was subsequently the superintendent of Baron Van de Cappelan's plantation on the Island. The Indian massacre of 1655 drove him temporarily from the Island, but he soon returned, and resumed his residence here. His family consisted of his wife, five children and two servants. John, who was probably a grandson of Adrian, married Anna Housman, and they had the following sons baptized :

Abraham, April 19, 1748, and

Adrian, April 26, 1748.

Garret and Sarah Ellis had the following sons baptized:

Garret, August 7, 1754.

Abraham, March 12, 1758.

Abraham had a daughter Miriam, born July 31, 1790.

There was another Garret born 1720, and died March 31, 1797.

The notices of this family are very meagre.

PRALL.

The present representatives of the family are:

Hon. Benjamin P. Prall, of Huguenot, Westfield, and his brother Capt. Arthur Prall, of New Springville, Northfield.

Their father was Peter Prall, born 1763, and died Nov. 1, 1822; his father was Benjamin Prall, born 1733, and died 1796; his father was Abraham Prall, born 1706 and died Sep. 28, 1775; his father was Peter Prall, whose name we find recorded as a witness or sponsor at a baptism in 1708; he had an older son than Abraham, viz.: Arent born 1698, and a younger Isaac born 1710.

This brings us very near, or quite to the original of the family. There was, however, an Arent Prall, who probably was either father or brother of the last mentioned Peter. We find his—Arent's—name on record as owning 120 acres of land on Long Neck in 1694.

Other members of the family, not in the above line, were Peter, born Apr. 9, 1737, and died Feb. 28, 1822; his brother Abraham, born 1740, died May 6, 1820; he had two sons, viz. Daniel, drowned Oct. 10, 1817, and Ichabod, a merchant in New York; Daniel married Ann Mersereau Jan. 22, 1794.

Scattered through various records, we find the following, whom we are unable to place, viz.:

Aron, Jun., and his wife Antye Staats, had a daughter born May 21, 1715; a son Aron in 1717; a daughter in 1719, and a son Peter in 1724.

Aron, or Arent, (not Jun.) and his wife Maritje Bowman had a son William Joris, born 1730, and a son Hendrick, born 1735.

Isaac (probably the son of Abraham, above mentioned) and his wife Maria Debaa or Dubois, had a daughter born 1746, and another in 1748; a son Peter in 1744, and a son Lewis in 1751.

Benjamin and his wife Sarah Swaim had a son Abraham born in 1752, and a son John in 1766.

John (wife's name not given) had a daughter born in 1719.

Abraham and Sarah Cannon were married Aug. —, 1776.

John and Martha Latourette were married Jan. 14, 1802.

There was a Wolford Praule, who was a freeholder as early as 1695, but he was not probably connected with this family, as his name was spelled differently, and there is no further notice of him.

RYERSS.

We find this name at an early date on Long Island. Arie Ryerse and Maerte Ryerse were assessed as owners of property at Middelwout, now Flatbush, in 1676, but when their connection with Staten Island began is unknown.

Adrian was born 1715, and died December 12, 1779; his wife was Hester Debaa (Dubois;) their son Lewis was born December 7, 1754, and died April 13, 1806.

Aris, another son of Adrian, had a daughter baptized July 27, 1786, and a son David, baptized October 17, 1790.

Gozen, also a son of Adrian, made his will October 21, 1800, proved January 13, 1802, in which he speaks of his son John P., and his daughter Margaret, his brother Lewis, and his grandsons Gozen Adrian Ryers, and Ryerss De Hart.

He was an exceedingly obese man, and required two ordinary chairs to sit upon; his wife was in the same condition. He was a wealthy man, and owned property in various parts of the county. In 1791 he became the owner of 300 acres of land, in the eastern part of the State, which, when the line between New York and Massachusetts was finally determined, fell within the latter State. To compensate him for the loss of this land, the State of New York gave him a patent for 1800 acres in Wilmington Township, Essex County, which is

known as Ryerss' grant to this day. He dwelt for many
years preceding his death at Port Richmond, in the large
house known as the Continental Hotel. He was a very prominent and useful man ; he was supervisor of Northfield from
1785 to 1787 ; a member of the Constitutional Convention in
1788 ; he was Member of Assembly from 1791 to 1794, and
first Judge of the County from 1797 to his death.   His
brother Lewis was sheriff in 1788 –'90, and Member of Assembly from 1795 to 1797.   His son John P. was a Member of
Assembly 1800.

Probably the only remaining member of the family on the
Island is Mr. David R. Ryerss, living near the Moravian
Church.

SEGUINE.

We have been unsuccessful in our efforts to obtain reliable
information with regard to the origin of this family, and are
obliged to be content with such as can be found in the local
records, the earliest of which is—

Jean and Elizabeth Hooper, had a son Jonas, bap. Dec. 12,
1725.

Jaques and Lady Mambrut, daughter Sara, bap. Mar. 3,
1728.

A son Jean, bap. Mar. 19, 1732.

Jean and Jaques stood sponsors for each other's children ;
they were probably brothers.   The above are from the records
of the Dutch Church ; the following are from those of St.
Andrews :

James and Elsee, daughter Sara, born Apr., 1756.

Son James, born Dec. 10, 1760.

John and Sarah had the following children :

Elisha, born May 31, 1760.

James bap. July 18, 1762.

Henry, born Feb. 4, 1764.

Lawrence and Ann, daughter Sara, born Apr. 2, 1761.

James and Caty, son Stephen, born Mar. 22, 1764.

Son James, born Apr. 5, 1766.

James made his will June 13, 1795, proved Oct. 7, 1795; mentions his wife Catharine and his children Barnt, Joseph, Frederick, John, Henry, Stephen and James.

John and Rachel Mitchel married Nov. —, 1775.

John and Margaretta, son John, bap. Oct. 24, 1790.

Son Henry, bap. Oct. 27, 1793.

James and Mary Guyon married June 30, 1791.

Stephen and Susanna Poillon married Nov. 8, 1792.

Henry and Jane Garretson married Aug. 18, 1800.

Stephen and Margaret Guyon married Mar. 5, 1805.

SHARROTT.

This is another example of the change of a French name into English.

Richard Sharet, the first of the name on Staten Island, according to the family traditions and records, was a Frenchman by birth, of Huguenot parentage, and for a short period after his emigration resided in New England. He came to Staten Island either just before, or just after, the commencement of the Revolution. Here he married a woman of German parentage named Mary Heger. Their children were William, Richard, John, James, Susan and Mary.

John married Mary Ann Burbank. October 9th, 1789 ;

their children were Peter, (died Feb., 1875, aged 86,) John, Jeremiah, Richard, Abraham, William Henry, Mary, Susan, Catharine, Eliza, Louisa—some of whom are still living.

SIMONSON.

This name was found in the province as early as 1631. Willem came over in the "Fox" in 1662, and was probably the first of the name on Staten Island. The family has become so numerous during the past two centuries that it is impossible at this day to ascertain whether the several branches are of kin or not. The branch descended from Barnt appears to have been the most prolific.

Barnt and Apollonia Messeker had a daughter bap. in 1701 ; a son John in 1702, and a son Aart in 1710.

Aert (Arthur) and Margaret Daniels had the following children :

Simon, bap. Apr. 20, 1708.
Hans, (John) bap. ——, 1710.
Aert, bap. Oct. 11, 1711, died in infancy.
Aert, bap. July 14, 1718.
Christopher, bap. June 18, 1714.
Daniel, bap. July 26, 1724.
Barnt, bap. July 14, 1728.

* Simon (above) and Sarah Van Pelt had the following children:

Van Pelt, bap. Mar. 18, 1742.
Aert, bap. May 21, 1744.
John, bap. May 2, 1754.
Evert, bap. Dec. 18, 1755.

* These were probably members of another branch of the original family, descended from Aert or Arthur.

Hans, (above) and Antje (dim. of Ann) Van Pelt, daughter bap. June 7, 1743.

Christofel, (Christopher above,) and Maria Van Shurze had a son Christofel, bap. Apr. 19, 1748.

Hans, (above) was probably the husband of Suster Corsen; he was a constable in 1770.

Daniel and Maria Decker had a son Abraham, bap. Feb. 26, 1758; a daughter in 1752, and another daughter in 1754.

Isaac and Neeltje (Cornelia) Coteleau, had a son Isaac, bap. Dec. 17, 1732; this Isaac was the father of Joseph, who married Elizabeth Winant, and they were the parents of the following sons: John, Jacob and David, still living at New Springville; Joseph, still living at Graniteville, and Abraham, deceased, also of the wife of Hon. John B. Hillyer.

Cornelius and Elizabeth Depue, had son Barnt, bap. June 24, 1759.

Daniel and Molly Decker had son Abraham, bap. Feb. 26, 1758.

* Isaac and Antje (dim. of Ann) Vanderbilt, daughter bap. July 8, 1722.

Christofel and Catarina Van Scuren, had daughter bap. May 6, 1748.

Isaac had a daughter Elizabeth, bap. Aug. 30, 1789.

Jacob and Adra Poillon were married Jan. 22, 1790; he was born in 1768, and died Oct. 27, 1844, in his 76th year; she was born June 5, 1765, and died July 10, 1871, aged 106 years, 1 mo. 5 days; they had a daughter Elizabeth, bap. May 1, 1791, and a son John P., born Oct. 18, 1810, and died June 20, 1868; he lived in Heberton Street, Port Richmond.

Barnt and Abigail Crocheron, married Mar. 8, 1755.

Barnt and Abigail, had a son John, born July 17, 1758.

John and Ann, daughter Frances, born Dec. 26, 1771; son John, born Dec. 6, 1773.

Isaac and Elizabeth Wood, married July 28, 1757.

Isaac and Elizabeth Bird married Apr. 5, 1789.

John and Alice Marshal, married Jan. 5, 1790.

* These were also probably members of another branch of the original famil descended from Aert or Arthur.

Peter and Ann Côle, married Aug. 20, 1791.

John and Phebe Wood, married Sep. 28, 1799.

*Arthur and Harriet Pritchard, married June 27, 1801.

* Charles M., born 1780, died July 26, 1858; he lived at Stapleton.

Reuben, born Jan. 1765, died Sep. 19, 1844.

John, born Apr. 15, 1782, died Nov. 25, 1862.

Isaac made his will June 28, 1787; proved July 9, 1787; mentions his wife Helethay, and his sons Jeremiah and Isaac; no other children mentioned.

There was another Isaac, born October 2, 1761, died May 17, 1855, in his 94th year.

STILWELL.

Of English origin. The family was here at an early date. The first mention of the name, with reference to the Island, is in the Albany records, where a piece of wood-land on the south side of Fresh Kill is mentioned as belonging to Daniel Stilwell in 1680. There is also mention made in our county records of Richard in 1689; of John in 1695 –'6 and 1708, and of Thomas in 1697 and 1704. It would appear then that at the close of the 17th century there were at least four families of the name in the county. We subjoin the names of those found in the several church records.

Elias and his wife Anne Burbank, (she was probably the daughter of Thomas Burbank and Maritje Martling. See Burbank family,) had a son Thomas baptized June 30, 1726, and a son Daniel baptized March 24, 1728. Thomas married Debora Martling, and had a son Elias baptized June 10, 1747.

* These were also probably members of another branch of the original family, descended from Aert or Arthur.

Daniel, whose wife's name was Annatje (Anna,) had a daughter Susannah, baptized July 18th, 1762. There was another Daniel whose wife was Maria Poillon, who had a son Jaques baptized March 26, 1788, and a son Daniel, baptized April 4, 1786, whose wife's name was Ariantje, and had a son Jeremiah, born December 1, 1768.

. Here we abandon the attempt further to trace the genealogy, and give the remaining names which we have collected, leaving it to the members of the family to discover their own ancestors.

Sarah Pareyn (Perine,) wife of William "*obiit,*" had twins William and Daniel, baptized September 6, 1719.—(Posthumous.)

Jan and Elizabeth Parein (Perine) had a son John, baptized November 15, 1719.

Thomas and Sarah Van Name had a son Thomas, baptized December 22, 1728.

Daniel and Catharine Larzalere had a son Richard, baptized November 25, 1739.

Joachim and Anna Tenners had a son John, baptized July 28, 1751, and a son Richard, May 23, 1759.

Thomas and Nancy Fountain had a son Antone, baptized February 16, 1755.

John and Helena Van Name had a son Elias baptized June 24, 1752.

Richard and Jenneke (Jane) Van Name had a son Nicholas, baptized September 21, 1785.

The above are from the records of the Dutch Church; the following are from St. Andrews.

Nicholas (son of last mentioned Richard) and his wife Effey (Eva) had a daughter Catharine, born November 18, 1761.

Jeremiah and his wife Yetty had a son Peter, born April 30th, 1764.

John and Olly Taylor were married September 15, 1757.

Samuel and Hannah Van Pelt were married June 9, 1755.

Richard and Mary his wife had a son Daniel, born February 7, 1770.

Nicholas born Jan. ——, 1747; died April 26, 1819.

Abraham born Mar. 1750; died Sep. 12, 1824.

The Stilwells were for a long time an influential and prominent family in the county, and members of it filled many local offices; (see civil and military lists,) while there are yet several highly respectable individuals among them; one branch has physically, morally, and intellectually deteriorated.

SPRAGUE.

The tradition in the family is that there were three brothers, Joseph, Edward and John, emigrated simultaneously from England, but the date of that event is lost; it must have been early, however, as we read of Jacob Spragg, who must have been a son of Joseph, as early as 1729. Of these brothers, Joseph took up his abode on Staten Island; of the other two, one settled on Long Island, and one on Rhode Island. William, whose name we find in the county records in 1767, and Joseph in 1772, were undoubtedly grandsons of the original Joseph. The original Joseph had three sons—Jacob, John and Edward—notwithstanding, the family has not increased very rapidly, and at present number but a few families, mostly confined to the town of Westfield. The only notices of the name in the old record of St. Andrew's Church, are the following:

Andrew and Catharine Pryor married June 28, 1800.

Jacob and Margaret Wood married July 12, 1800.

TAYLOR.

Abraham and Harmintje Haughwout had the following children :

Son Ephraim, bap. Oct. 28, 1711, died young.

Daughter Altje, (Alida) bap. May 18, 1710, died young.

Daughter Rachel, bap. Aug. 21, 1720.

Daughter Altje, bap. Nov. 25, 1722.

Son Peter, bap. July 4, 1725.

Son Ephraim, bap. Apr. 6, 1729.

Daughter Margaret, bap. Nov. 28, 1715.

Ephraim married Elizabeth Morgan, Jan. 4, 1756.

Another Ephraim, probably father of Abraham, had a son Jan, and a daughter Marietta, both bap. in 1696.

The above family, though English in name, had assimilated with the Dutch, as is evident from the names of some of them, and are found in the records of the Dutch Church. The following are found in the records of St. Andrew's Church, and are of another family.

Oliver, born 1687, and died Aug. 24, 1771 ; there is nothing to indicate that he was born on the Island, though he died here.

Henry and Judith had a son John, born Sept. 20, 1770.

Oliver and Sarah, daughter Elisabeth, born Aug. 24, 1771.

Henry and Lydia, son Abraham, bap. ———, 1775.

John and Fanny, son Oliver, born Sept. 24, 1791.

Benjamin and Ann Decker married Sept. 9, 1792.

John and Sarah Yates married Jan. 7, 1804.

TOTTEN.

We can scarcely consider this family as among the old

families of the Island, though the name is found in local records for more than a century. In the records of St. Andrew's Church, the name occurs two or three times, until the
organization of the Methodist church, when it becomes identified with that church. Gilbert was one of the first, and
leading men, connected with that society.

The residence of the families bearing the name has been
almost exclusively in the town of Westfield, and the thriving
village of Tottenville in that town perpetuates their respecta-
bility and influence. The only notices of the name in church
records, other than those of the Méthodist church, are as
follows:

Silas and Charity his wife, had the following sons:

Joseph, born Aug. 10, 1765.

Ephraim, born Feb. 24, 1768.

Joseph and Mary Cubberly married Dec. 11, 1804.

Though the family appear to have always maintained a
very respectable position, they do not appear to have been
aspirants for political distinction; Ephraim, Gilbert and
John, have repeatedly served their town as supervisors, and
Ephraim J., was Member of Assembly in 1848.

VAN BUSKIRK, VAN DUZER.

Neither of these can be regarded as old Staten Island
families. There was a Cornelius Van Buskirk here during
the Revolution, but he came from Bergen. The sites of the
Pavilion at New Brighton, and St. Peter's Church, occupy a
part of his farm. His dwelling house stood along the Shore
Road, at the foot of the hill upon which St. Mark's Hotel
stands, and is alluded to elsewhere. He had a son who

owned a farm on the road leading from Quarantine to Richmond, near the Clove road. Another son lived at West New Brighton, near Pine, Hillyer & Co's store, and owned the mill which formerly stood on the "Factory Dock ;" his wife was a Schermerhorn, from Schenectady.

The Van Buskirks were among the earliest settlers on Bergen Point, and were a very respectable, though not a numerous family, on the Island. The venerable Mrs. Van Duzer, mother-in-law of Hon. H. B. Metcalfe, now (June, 1876,) in her 96th year, but since deceased, married a son of the original Cornelius Van Buskirk, and after his death married the late Daniel Van Duzer.

The Van Duzer family originally came from Long Island, and settled on Staten Island near the close of the last century. They were never very numerous.

Daniel Van Duzer left, at least, two sons—John H., for many years a baker at Tompkinsville, and Daniel C., a grocer at the same place, both now deceased.

VANDERBILT.

Jacob, the first of the name on Staten Island, was a native of Flatbush, Long Island, and was the son of Aris and Hilitje his wife. On the 19th of May, 1715, Aris sold a large tract of land at New Dorp to his son Jacob, who came to reside upon it. See *Note*, at the end of this article.

Jacob was born Jan. 25th, 1692, and died 1759; his wife Elenor, or Neiltje, was born Feb. 10th, 1698; their children were :

Aris, born Feb. 2, 1716.
Denys, born Sept. 5, 1717.
Hilitje, born Mar. 22, 1720.

Jacob, born Jan. 6, 1723.

Magdalena, born Dec. 1, 1725, married Cornelius Ellis.

John, born Nov. 15, 1728.

Cornelius, born Sept. 22, 1731.

Anna, born Feb. 11, 1734.

Phebe, born Apr. 27, 1737.

Anthea, born Jan. 31, 1739.

Elenor, born Sept. 13, 1742.

Jacob (born Jan. 6, 1723) married Mary Sprague, who was born Feb. 17, 1729 ; their children were :

Elenor, born ———, 1747, married a Johnson.

Jacob, born Jan. 6, 1750.

John, born May 9, 1752.

Dorothy, born July 29, 1754, married a Swaim.

Oliver, born June 16, 1757.

Joseph, born Sept. 6, 1761.

Cornelius, born Aug. 28, 1764.

Cornelius (born Aug. 28, 1764) married Phebe Hand, who was born April 15, 1767. He died May 20, 1832 ; she died June 22, 1854 ; their children were :

Mary, born Dec. 21, 1787, married Chas. M. Simonson, died Aug. 10, 1845.

Jacob, born Aug. 28. 1789, died Oct. 3, 1805.

Charlotte, born Dec. 29, 1791, married Capt. John De Foreest, died Jan. 5, 1877.

Cornelius, born May 27, 1794 (the Commodore), died Jan. 4, 1877.

Phebe, born Feb. 19, 1798, died young.

Jane, born Aug. 1, 1800, married—1st, Van Duzer ; 2d, Col. Saml. Barton.

Elenor, born Jan. 4, 1804, died Apr. 21, 1833.

Jacob Hand, born Sept. 2, 1807.

Phebe, born Feb. 9, 1810.

Another branch of the family is as follows :

John, who was member of Assemby in 1829, was the son of Jacob, who we are unable to place. John was born Aug. 1, 1769, and died Mar. 27, 1851 ; his sons were : John, born

July 2, 1796, died Aug. 13, 1847; Oliver, Aaron, Edward, Cornelius, Richard, Jacob. John and Oliver were well known in their day as captains of steamboats, the former on the line between Elizabethport and New York; the latter between New York and Staten Island, and other places.

Note.—Beside the land which Jacob bought of his father Aris, he purchased a parcel adjoining the above from Nathaniel Britton and Elizabeth his wife, on the 4th day of May, 1719, which was a part of a tract of 100 acres granted to Nathaniel Britton, father of the above named grantor, by Benjamin Fletcher, then Governor of the province, on the 25th day of June, 1696.

VAN NAME.

This is one of the old Dutch families of the county, but not among the oldest. The earliest mention of the name occurs in a church record, as follows:

Evert and Wyntje (Wilhelmina) Benham had a son Joseph, bap. Apr. 22, 1709, and a daughter Aug. 3, 1718.

Simon and Sarah Prall had a daughter bap. Oct. 30, 1716.

A son Aaron, Aug. 17, 1718, and

A son Moses, Feb. 21, 1725.

Engelbert and Maria De Camp had a son John bap. Apr. 12, 1719, and twin daughters Oct. 15, 1721.

Johannes had a son Pieter, bap. May 18, 1718.

Aaron (son of Simon, above) and Mary McLean, had the following children: Aaron (grandfather of Michael and Charles of Mariner's Harbor), Catharine, Simon, William, Ann, Moses and Charles.

Aaron (last mentioned) had a son Moses, who married Mary Le Grange; they had the following children, named in the order of their births: John, Polly, Moses, Elizabeth, Catharine, *Michael*, Sophia, Rachel, *Charles* and Aaron. Those in Italics are still living, 1877.

There was another Moses, born Feb., 1760, died Oct. 16, 1811; Simon, born Feb., 1739, died Nov. 24, 1812.

Charles, of another branch of the family, made his will Apr. 8, 1805, probated May 21, 1805, in which he mentions his sons Anthony and Aaron, both minors.

VAN PELT.

We read of individuals of this name in New Utrecht, several years before we meet the name in connection with Staten Island: thus, Wouter (Walter), Anthony, and Aert Van Pelt, are mentioned as early as 1687, living on Long Island. The first Van Pelt we meet in the Staten Island records is Hendrick, who had several children born between 1696 and 1701. He was, probably, connected with the Long Island families, as we find their names perpetuated on Staten Island. At, or about, the same time, there was a Peter Van Pelt, who had a son Jan baptized Oct. 21, 1707, and a son Samuel July 25, 1710.

This John and Jannetje (Janet) Adams, his wife, had

A daughter ——, bap. March 28, 1736.

A son William, April 13, 1742, and

A daughter ——, April —, 1744.

Jacob and Aaltje (Alida) Haughwout, his wife, had

A son John, baptized October 15, 1727.

A daughter Catalyntje, September 27, 1724.

John and Susanna Latourette, his wife, had twins—

John and Susanna, baptized May 25, 1729.

Tunis and Maria Drageau, his wife, had the following children:

Son Anthony, baptized October 9, 1729.

Son Johannes, baptized February 14, 1731.

Daughter Maria, baptized June 8, 1734.

Son Joost, baptized May 19, 1737.

Son Tunis, baptized November 19, 1738.

Peter had a son William, baptized November 28, 1715; a son Samuel, April 16, 1717.

Simon and Maria Adams had a

Son Peter, baptized May 28, 1749, and a

Daughter, April 18, 1748.

John (Anthony's son) and Susanna Latourette, his wife, had

A son Joost, baptized April 4, 1736, and

A son Anthony, baptized April 30, 1738.

This Anthony married Janneke Simonson, and had

A daughter ———, baptized June 11, 1760.

Peter and Barber Houlton had

A daughter ———, baptized April 18, 1748, and

A son David, baptized October 12, 1755.

Jan and Maria Bouman had a daughter, baptized September 14, 1742.

Jan, Jr. and Catrina Bouman had a daughter, baptized May 6, 1745.

John had a daughter, baptized October 29, 1787.

Samuel, son of Peter, mentioned above, and Maria Falkenburg, had

A son Pieter, baptized July 19, 1748.

Aart and Christina Immet, daughter Maria, baptized December 10, 1721.

John and Margaret, his wife, had the following children:—

A son Tunis, born August 8, 1760.

A son John, born February 10, 1765.

A son James, born May 18, 1761, and

A son Peter, born November 18, 1769.

Peter and Phebe had a son Tunis, born June 6, 1768.

Anthony and Susanna had a daughter Susanna, born May 10, 1766, and

A son George, born Mar. 1, 1769.

Joseph and Elizabeth had son James, born Aug. 5, 1767, and

A son Tunis, born Dec. 2, 1771.

John and Catharine Lawrence, daughter Mary, baptized March 8, 1772.

Jacob and Elizabeth, daughter Mary, born March 11, 1768.

Peter, son of John and Margaret, above, married Mary Colon, December 5, 1797.

David and Hannah Wright married June 21, 1801. He was born February ——, 1779, and died March 30, 1838.

There is a tradition that one of the earliest Van Pelt's, probably Hendrick, was a man of immense size ; he was very tall, and proportionately bulky, and possessed of strength equal to that of several ordinary individuals.

The Indians, who, notwithstanding their repeated sales of the Island, continued to prowl over it, pilfering from the settlers whatever they could lay their hands upon, were much afraid of him, and kept themselves far away from his premises. He had a son who was a dwarf in stature, not exceeding four feet in height, who was the constant companion of his father ; they were, in fact, inseparable in the day time. When the father died, the son took to his bed, and died two days thereafter.

WANDEL.

The first of the name in our county records is John, who, with his wife Letitia, executed a mortgage to —— Groom, May 1, 1767, and cancelled it by payment the next year. He was a cordwainer by trade, and carried on the tanning business on Toad Hill. John and Letitia had a son Peter born

January 10th, 1766. Peter married Sarah Van Clief, March
——, 1789, and died May 17th, 1857, over 91 years of age.
His sons were Matthew, Daniel, John, Peter S., and Walter
I., the latter only still living, April, 1876.

————

WINANT.

This is one of the oldest families on the Island, and is so
ramified that it is impossible to trace all its branches to their
sources. We select that branch which is probably best
known, and is represented by Abraham, and his brother
Jacob G., both of whom have been sheriffs of the county.
They are the sons of Hon. Bornt Parlee Winant, who is still
living at Rossville. His parents were Abraham Winant and
Mary Parlee, who were married August 1, 1807. The father
of Abraham was Winant Winant, who made his will July
5th, 1804, which was proved Aug. 11th, 1804, between which
dates he must have died. In that instrument he mentions
his wife Mary, and his children Abraham, John G., Jacob
G., Mary, Frances and Ann. The father of Winant Winant
was Abraham, who was the son of the elder Winant Winant,
who was the son of Peter Winant, the progenitor of the
family. The following is the inscription upon his tombstone:

"Here lies the body of Peter Winant, born in the year
1654, who departed this life August 6th, 1758, aged 104 years."

He was a native of Holland, but the date of his emigration
and settlement on the Island, which are identical, has been lost.

As his family was the only one of the name then in the
county, the following must have been his sons, viz.:

Peter, who had a son Peter, baptized April 23d, 1707.

Winant (mentioned above), whose wife was Ann Cole, who

had the following sons baptized: Peter, Mar. 27, 1720 ; Abraham, Mar. 24th, 1725 ; Jacob, Oct. 9th, 1726, and Daniel,
Apr. 22, 1728.

John, whose wife was Lena Bird, had a son Peter baptized
Mar. 19, 1732 ; and

Cornelius, whose wife was Maria Cole, had a son Cornelius
baptized Feb. 28th, 1728.

The following are other members of the family, whose
names we find in the county and church records:

Capt. Peter, born Dec. 4, 1784; he was captain of the
schooner Thames, which was wrecked on Absecom beach,
Nov. 4, 1823, when he lost his life.

Peter, born Oct. 5th, 1802, died Feb. 8, 1867.

Abraham and Mary his wife had a daughter Ann, born
Sep. 30, 1758, and a daughter Elizabeth, born Mar. 3, 1770.

Daniel and Rachel his wife had a son Daniel, born May 10,
1760.

Daniel and Susannah his wife had a daughter Ann, born
June 27, 1762.

Daniel and Elizabeth his wife had a daughter Rachel, born
Oct. 4, 1765.

Peter and Christiana his wife had a son George, born Sep.
6, 1770 ; this George married Eliza Winant, Nov. 15, 1794.

John and Hannah, or Johanna his wife, had a daughter
Elizabeth, born July 29, 1774, and a son Jacob, May 15, 1776.

Peter and Charity his wife had a son Isaac, born Feb. 1,
1775 ; this Isaac married Patty Winant, Jan. 16, 1796.

Peter and Ann his wife had two children, Daniel and
Ann, baptized Nov. 20, 1785. See *Note* below.

Cornelius, and Catharine his wife, had a daughter Cornelia
baptized Nov. 21, 1790.

Peter and Mary Winant were married July 14, 1790.

Moses and Catharine Winant were married Aug. 7, 1800.

Daniel and Eliza Oakley were married Dec. 19, 1801.

Note.—Peter Winant made his will May 9, 1793, which was proved
July 26, 1793, in which he mentions his wife Ann, his father Daniel,
and alludes to his children without giving their names.

WOGLOM.

This name was originally written "Van Wogelum."

John sold land in 1696; this is the earliest mention of the name in the local records; the next is—

Grysie Woggelum, who was witness at a baptism in 1698.

John Van W. had daughter Chrystyntien, bap. 22, 1707, and a daughter Suster, bap. July 26, 1711.

Ary (Adrian) and Celia Pryer had the following children:

Son Jan, bap, May 21, 1716.

Daughter Anna, bap. June 3, 1722.

Son Andries, bap. June 27, 1725.

Son Adrian, bap. July 27, 1729.

Son Abraham, bap. Aug. 8, 1731.

There was a Douwe Van W. residing on the Island in 1742.

The next notices of any members of the family are from the records of St. Andrews.

Abraham and Hannah Parlee, married Nov. 18, 1790.

Joshua and Martha Cole married Feb. 10, 1796.

John and Lanah Pryor married Dec. 24, 1808.

WOOD.

This family is of English origin. The name is common everywhere, and it is exceedingly doubtful whether the Woods on the Island have descended from the same original. The present representative of one of the families is Samuel B. Wood, Esq., residing near Garrison's Station, on the S. I. Railroad. He is the son of the late John B., who, with his brother Samuel (still living 1876), are the sons of Samuel. Samuel's brothers were Joseph, John, Stephen and Jesse, and they were the sons of John, the g. grandfather of Samuel B., Esq. It is impossible to trace the genealogy of any other branch, but subjoin the names of such as are to be found in the several church records.

Stephen and his wife Geertje (Gertrnde) Winter, had twins Stephen and Obadia, baptized Dec. 24, 1727.

Stephen and his wife Jemima Mott had a son Richard, baptized June 13, 1731.

The above are from the records of the Dutch Church; the following are from those of St. Andrew's Church.

Stephen and Mary his wife had a daughter, Mary, born Sept. 18, 1772; a son Stephen, bap. June 5, 1785.

John and Margaret his wife had a son Stephen, bap. Aug. 1, 1773, who married Damy Housman Feb. 3, 1794. (This Stephen was one of the five brothers mentioned above as sons of John.)

Stephen and Alice, or Elsy, his wife, had a son John, bap. June 15, 1783; he married Barbara Van Pelt Dec. 23, 1804, and another son, Abraham, born Sep. 22, 1788.

Timothy and Sarah Rezeau were married Jan. —, 1769.

Isaac and Susan Lewis were married Feb. 9, 1794.

John and Sarah Lockman were married Mar. 23, 1794.

Richard and Catharine Lockman were married Jan. 7, 1795.

James and ———— Elston (Alston ?) were married June 1, 1799.

Charles and Joanna Dongan were married Dec. 11, 1806.

(She was the daughter of the late Walter Dongan, of the Four Corners, and the mother of Mr. Walter D. Wood, of Mariner's Harbor.)

Jesse and Catharine Marshal were married July 9, 1807.

James, mentioned above, lived at Long Neck, or Travisville, and his sons were Charles, mentioned above, John, Peter and Abraham; Charles was well known in his day as a local preacher in the Methodist Church.

John, brother of Charles, married Mary Jones, and was the father of James, deceased in 1831, and Edward resides at Travisville.

www.ingramcontent.com/pod-product-compliance
Lightning Source LLC
Chambersburg PA
CBHW070929270326
41927CB00011B/2778